FOUNDATIONS

—— FOR THE ——

BATTLEFIELD

FOUNDATIONS
—— FOR THE ——
BATTLEFIELD

DAVID FALLS

CREATION
HOUSE
A STRANG COMPANY

FOUNDATIONS FOR THE BATTLEFIELD by David Falls
Published by Creation House
A Strang Company
600 Rinehart Road
Lake Mary, Florida 32746
www.strangbookgroup.com

Unless otherwise noted, all Scripture quotations are from the New American Standard Bible. Copyright © 1960, 1962, 1963, 1968, 1971, 1972, 1973, 1975, 1977 by the Lockman Foundation. Used by permission. (www.Lockman.org)

Scripture quotations marked NIV are from the Holy Bible, New International Version of the Bible. Copyright © 1973, 1978, 1984, International Bible Society. Used by permission.

Scripture quotations marked KJV are from the King James Version of the Bible.

The spelling and pronounciation of various Greek and Hebrew terms cited in this book have been taken from *Strong's Exhaustive Concordance of the Bible.*

Design Director: Bill Johnson
Cover design by Justin Evans

Library of Congress Control Number: 2009943071
International Standard Book Number: 978-1-61638-143-1

First Edition

10 11 12 13 — 9 8 7 6 5 4 3 2 1
Printed in the United States of America

CONTENTS

ACKNOWLEDGMENTS

FIRST I WOULD LIKE TO THANK MY LORD and Savior Jesus Christ without whom there would be no point in writing this book in the first place. Our situation would be hopeless, helpless, and very unpleasant without You.

Next comes my lovely wife, Wendy, who has faithfully offered her love, companionship, encouragement, and prodding to help me finish what I started. You were my first editor who suffered through my first draft without complaint. You have been with me every step of the way. I love you with all my heart.

There is Clinton and Connie Robertson who granted me encouragement, wisdom, and a whole other round of editing help, observations, and hand-holding. I can't thank you guys enough for all your support.

Then comes Hannah Pettingill who sacrificially gives of herself to my family and me on a continual basis. Our lives would not be what they are without you. You are a true friend. Thank you.

Thank you, ZHOP Charlotte, for a pleasant place to sit, pray, worship, and write. Without you guys, I wouldn't have had anywhere close to as much fun writing this book.

Lastly, I would like to thank all the folks at Creation House

(Virginia Maxwell, Atalie Anderson, Brenda Davis, Amanda Quain, and many others) for all the amazing things you do to make good books happen. Without your help I would have nothing more than an interesting stack of paper lying around the house. It never would have made it into the hands of the readers that it is intended to bless, and it certainly wouldn't be as good as it is today. Thank you all.

INTRODUCTION

THIS IS A BOOK ABOUT WAR. NOT A WAR FOUGHT with guns, planes, and bombs; those wars come and go. They are only the manifestation of a much greater conflict, one which has consumed humanity since the beginning of mankind. We did not start the fight. It was already ongoing. We were born into it, or rather we were created (in part) for it.

There is a fight more vicious and desperate than you could possibly imagine going on all around you. It is a spiritual war fought by spirits and by men. Its outcome will determine the destiny of the entire human race. Whether you like it or not, you have a part to play. This ebb and flow of the lesser skirmishes affects your day-to-day life, and though it may be hard to fathom, your day-to-day life affects them in return. This book is meant to clarify the history and nature of the overall conflict, the ways in which it affects us on a daily basis, and how we can make an impact on it.

To give the reader an idea of where I am coming from, let me start by sharing a little bit of my own story and how I became aware of the war. I was born into the world oblivious to the conflict going on all around me. I grew up in a relatively peaceful Christian household. We were churchgoers in an Assembly of God church. I couldn't tell you a whole lot about the church other than they believed in Jesus and did their best to follow Him. I remember the devil being talked about once in a while, but it was almost always in a sense that had to do with him being a tempter (like what we see in the Garden of Eden). I know my parents were aware of the verses in Ephesians that talk about us wrestling against spiritual beings and about Christians having spiritual armor. However, I don't think they really knew much about applying them. As far as I can tell, they did their utmost to follow the Lord, which resulted in all sorts of crazy adventures that could easily fill another book. Yet for the most part, they too were oblivious to the war we all live in.

I know that our family was affected by it every day, but we were never able to put two and two together. One day, one of my elementary schoolteachers called home to talk to my mother about my underperformance in her class. She began to explain to my mom that she thought that there was a real problem at the root of it. She noticed that I would seem to blank out quite frequently in the middle of her class. One minute I would be present, paying attention to what was going on, and the next minute I would be gone. My mom initially chalked it up to daydreaming and told me to pay more attention in class. My teacher wisely persisted and eventually talked my mom into getting me checked out by a doctor.

As it turns out, my pediatrician was a child neurological specialist who quickly realized that I had epilepsy. To confirm the diagnosis, I underwent an EEG a few days later. As it turns out, I was having regular seizures, which would cause me to lose consciousness without showing any physical signs except a very blank stare. I would come and go and not even be aware that a full minute or more had passed. Generally, these types of seizures are not considered very serious; most children outgrow them within a few years. In my case, however, I was having them at an extraordinary rate (several an hour). Let's put it this way: I was gone a total of 5 to 10 minutes an hour. I was considered to be one of those rare likely candidates in whom the epilepsy would progress into far more serious seizures as I got older. So I was assigned a regimen of anti-seizure medication to bring my seizures under control.

Within a few days of my diagnosis, my father's dear friend Bill came to visit. He was (and still is) the proverbial bachelor, only in his singleness he completely devoted himself to following the Lord. He developed a pattern in which he would volunteer full-time with a new ministry every few years. With each new ministry, he would learn and grow in his faith in the areas where they were strong. One day, he and my father went to lunch, and my father asked him the typical, "So what have you been up to?" Then Bill got all animated and started telling my dad about this deliverance ministry in which he'd just been involved. To better explain what he was talking about, he told this story of a woman who had a spirit of epilepsy cast out of her. It was one of those stories where the minister commanded the spirit to come out of her and it immediately took over the woman and started talking back to him. Eventually the spirit left, and she quit having epileptic seizures. Then my father remarked out loud, and mostly to himself, "Gee, my son has epilepsy."

"Great, we'll cast it out of him!" was Bill's immediate reply.

"Uh, I don't think so, Bill."

"Don't worry about it. We'll just kick it out of him, and he'll be fine."

"No, Bill, you don't understand. He's my son. I believe in demons (they're in the Bible). But, I don't have any experience with this sort of thing, and you're relatively new at it. I'm not going to let you experiment on my son." Eventually, Bill managed to convince my father that the matter was worth looking into.

My parents spent the next number of days pouring over reading materials that Bill had given them. Some of the books and pamphlets had lists of common symptoms for demonic infestation. My parents were shocked to realize that most of those symptoms applied to me. After praying and thinking about it for some time, they decided to set a date for my deliverance. All of this went on without my knowledge.

The appointed evening came, and I underwent a fairly messy deliverance. I remember quite vividly coughing as each demon came out. I also remember getting very simple visions of each one right before or after it was kicked out. The deliverance took place over two nights because the process was so exhausting for me; I couldn't handle doing all of it in one night. All in all, quite a few demons were kicked out of me, which left a lot of empty space. To fill in that new space, my sister suggested that we ask the Lord to fill it up personally. I remember my formal introduction to Him even more vividly than the formal good-byes to all the demons.

I remember us praying and asking Him to come in and

fill up every empty space, and then all of the sudden I felt this very powerful, warm wind pass right through me. The description that I gave my parents was almost verbatim what was in Acts 2:2: "And suddenly there came from heaven a noise like a violent rushing wind, and it filled the whole house where they were sitting." It would be years later that I would actually read the Book of Acts for the very first time. In the days that followed the infilling, my life was very much altered. My grades began to improve, I quit having seizures, and I remember feeling the presence and empowerment of God for days afterward. I was eight years old at the time.

Right after this, my parents started getting requests from other people in the church to do deliverance on them. I would sit in on those little meetings in our house and help discern the particular spirits that were afflicting people. I didn't really understand the problems that people where having, and I don't remember my parents including me during the initial interviews where people would explain what their struggles and issues were. If I had been there, I don't think I would have understood adult problems very well at the age of eight. What I remember quite clearly is everyone sitting in our den, praying over someone, and things coming to a standstill. Then people would ask the Lord, "What is the next spirit that needs to be dealt with?" I remember getting impressions, which I could usually explain in a few words (examples might include fear, fear of failing, lust, anger, or unforgiveness). This usually gave enough direction so that my parents could help the person get free of that particular spirit.

The household deliverance ministry my parents were

engaging in only lasted a few months. They quickly hit burnout, because the work was so demanding. They also were unintentionally beginning to stir up controversy in our church, which didn't believe that a Christian could have a demon. So as much from exhaustion as to preserve the unity of the local body, they quit the deliverance ministry.

Through all of my early encounters with the supernatural I came to realize a few things. God is real, and He is good. The devil is real, and he is bad. God is bigger than the devil, and even though God can squash the devil like a bug, for some reason our involvement in the process is required. Beyond that I had no idea how any of this worked. Thus, I acquired an insatiable thirst for knowledge concerning how the spiritual realms function.

I wanted to know how the demons do what they do. How do they think? What are they trying to accomplish and why? Why doesn't God just squash them all like bugs? I knew that battles raged in the spiritual realms between angels and demons, but how were they fought? What determined a winner and a loser? What happens to a demon when it is driven out? And so on and so forth.

Between my own personal deliverance and sitting in on the deliverances of others, I learned that we have authority over the devil. This was wonderful. It took all fear out of the equation, but I still had far more questions than answers. I knew that for everything that I saw there was a whole lot more going on that I did not see. I was never content just to cast a few spirits out of a few tormented people. I wanted to affect the battle on a much grander scale. So I began to seek the Lord for a much greater understanding.

First I turned to books. Over the course of about a decade I read every book I could find that had anything to do with the supernatural, provided that they were basing their conclusions on the Word of God. I also began devouring the Word itself. I would spend hours asking the Lord questions about obscure passages of Scripture. The encouraging part is that He would answer me, sometimes on the spot and more often by dropping a book in my lap by someone who had spent years studying whatever obscure topic I was interested in.

I began to notice a pattern in the literature available about spiritual warfare. Usually an author would have an experience, and out of that experience the Lord would grant the author a substantial revelation about some element of the topic. Then the author would realize that the revelation could be of some value to the body, so he or she would write a book on it. In writing the book, the author would usually only explain the generalities of warfare to a depth that was necessary to substantiate and communicate his or her revelation. I believe that this happened this way for two reasons. On one hand, the author's purpose was to impart a particular revelation, so the rest of their understanding about warfare was extraneous. On the other hand, at the time, much of the understanding about warfare was in its infancy. Deliverance ministry was almost entirely lost to the church until just a couple of decades ago. There has been much to relearn. In any event, it was possible for someone like me to come along and read several very high quality books and still not have a meaningful holistic understanding of spiritual warfare.

I had to deal with one major objection from those I was close to. Many people in the body have this largely unfounded fear that by studying the devil and focusing on him so much, you can open yourself to become deceived by him. This can happen if you make the devil your focus and if your major tool for discernment is your natural mind. The carnal (natural) mind is not very good at grasping spiritual truth (Rom. 8:6–7; 1 Cor. 3). I made a point of asking the Lord (the source of all truth) to teach me, and I learned that He will not lead His own children into deception.

It wasn't until I went to college over a decade later that I started getting chances to test all that I was learning. Most colleges have a pretty hefty degree of darkness over them for a couple of reasons. The major one is that most college faculties deliberately foster an atmosphere of tolerance toward almost any form of experimentation, which inevitably encourages the doctrines of demons and continuous exposure to sin. Also, the most common outlook among faculty is one of secular humanism, and they pass it on to their students. Too often colleges operate under a godless system, where morals and truth are relative. In the name of respect for all beliefs, most every expression is tolerated—if not encouraged. I'm all about respect, but a line must be drawn somewhere. In the absence of standards and boundaries, colleges end up with an atmosphere in which the demonic can very easily work on those who are in attendance.

The college I went to had an added bonus. Next door to our little college town was a slightly smaller town that was populated almost entirely by witches and spiritualists. The influence of the occult was so strong that no ministry had ever successfully planted a church within its borders. In our town, witches would try to slip into the services unnoticed and put curses on people during the worship and altar ministry times. Sadly, many of the townspeople where either unaware of this activity or uncaring, because they thought it was all just a bunch of superstitious nonsense. Not surprisingly, church splits were common in the town. It was said that most of the town's one hundred-plus churches were founded because of church splits instead of healthy church growth.

In addition to acquiring a BS in physics and an MBA, I spent quite a bit of time studying and confronting the evil around me. When I wasn't studying or hanging out with my friends for fun, I was teaching them how to fight in the spirit. My relationship with the Lord grew tremendously during that time. We saw plenty of territorial warfare and personal deliverance. I endured countless spiritual assaults by witches praying against my friends and me. By the end of my senior year, my knowledge base from my countless hours of study had become eclipsed by my new experience base.

For the next several years, I went back to studying the Word to fill in some missing pieces and to try to better understand scripturally what I had encountered. In the last couple of years, the Lord has been leading me back into ministry to help others who have been through some extreme warfare but lacked the understanding to be able to overcome what the enemy had been throwing at them. It has given me a chance to witness firsthand the effectiveness of what all the Lord has been teaching me all these years.

In all, I have spent just shy of two decades seeking the understanding that I now possess. I have never encountered a book or series of books that could explain, to my satisfaction, a solid understanding of the foundations and functions of spiritual warfare. I seem to regularly encounter people who are in the place that I was so many years ago: they have had some encounter with both God and the demonic, and they know that they need to learn to confront their unseen foe while leaning on their unseen ally. But they have absolutely no idea what they are doing, so they stumble along as if in the darkness and begin to make very slow and painful progress. Then they start doing research, just like I did, and each book seems to add only a small piece of the puzzle. After reading two or three very different books on the topic, it becomes difficult to put together all the very different revelations into one coherent body of understanding.

My hope is that this book will give you a meaningful understanding of the war. By the end of the first half of this book you will understand the history of the struggle and the perspectives of both God and the devil. The second half is devoted to understanding the principles and mechanics of warfare itself. It opens with a two-chapter discussion on the nature of authority, how it works, and how our enemy usurps it. Then you will see in great detail how the different ranks of the demonic work and learn some effective strategies to use against each of them. Also, we will cover the basics of how witchcraft works against the believer and some appropriate ways to render it ineffective. The epilogue will cover the final outcome of the war and how it will happen.

To keep the book from being unnecessarily long and to fit the maximum amount of information into this volume, I have avoided repetition whenever possible. This means that if you really want to learn all of the information that is covered, then you may have to read this book more than one time. This calls for discipline on the part of the reader.

My sincere hope is that upon finishing this book you will find yourself with a much clearer understanding of what is going on around you in the spirit and what you can do about it.

Peace in Him,
David Falls

PART I

Chapter 1

IN THE BEGINNING

In the beginning God created the heavens and the earth. Now the earth was formless and empty, darkness was over the surface of the deep, and the Spirit of God was hovering over the waters.
—GENESIS 1:1–2, NIV

ORIGINALLY, THERE WAS NO BATTLE, NO CONTEST, no strife, only God creating. Yet in the above verse, I see one apparent contradiction: our God is a God of light. He is radiant. When Jesus was transfigured, He glowed so brightly He was painful to look at (Matt. 17:1–17). The prophet Ezekiel had an encounter with the Lord, and in his description, he includes the words *fire, lightning, bright,* and *brightness* more than ten times (Ezek. 1:4–28). The psalmist says that the hills melt like wax at His presence (Ps. 97:5). Yet the earth is dark.

If we read on, we see another quizzical thing. If you are reading from the King James translation there is a spot where God looks at His creation and says, "Be fruitful, and multiply, and replenish the earth" (Gen. 1:28). I got curious about that word *replenish* one day, so after some research I discovered that, sure enough, the word in Hebrew actually means "replenish." "But how can that be?" I wondered. *Replenish* is like saying "refill." In other words, fill it again. How can the earth be filled again with life when life has never existed before?

I contend that the earth was not originally created as an empty ball dwelling in darkness. Because of the Lord's nature, I believe He initially created the earth as a place teeming with life and filled with His light, and somehow the earth ended up barren and dark. I later discovered that many others had already stumbled on some of these apparent contradictions and concluded the same thing. This approach to Scripture is commonly called the Gap Theory.[1] We read the first verse of Genesis like this: "In the beginning God created the heavens and the earth." Then some unknown amount of time passed, a.k.a., the gap; at the end of that time we find that, "the earth is formless and empty."

So what happened during the gap?

Along with the heavens, the Lord created His angels. In general, these are very powerful beings created to love and serve Him. One of the most powerful and magnificent of these beings was named Lucifer.

At some point, Lucifer decided that He wanted to have God's throne and rule the cosmos (Isa. 14:13). He rebelled against his Creator, failed, was removed from the Lord's pres-

---

1 There are a few variations on the Gap Theory. One version states that Satan fell from heaven and converted some pre-Adamic race to his own desires, and they became known as demons. I am not, personally, a fan of the pre-Adamic race part of the theory, because I have never found any significant justification for it in Scripture.

ence, and was cast down to Earth along with his cohorts (v. 12). After arriving on Earth, Lucifer and his followers made a mess of everything (vv. 16–17).

At a later time, God decided to clean up their mess by recreating the earth. Because Lucifer was allowed to maintain his existence, his fight against the Lord would continue. In the midst of this fight, God created man, and the war took some very unfortunate turns. Before we search deeper into God's remedy, let's explore the true nature of Lucifer's rebellion and the battlefield this created.

Chapter 2

FROM LUCIFER TO SATAN

W E HAVE ESTABLISHED THAT THE EARTH WAS created, fell into darkness, was recreated, and is now embroiled in a war. To truly understand the character of this war, we need to have a firm grasp on why and how it started, where it is today, and what we are fighting toward.

I have discovered something about our God. He likes to say things in a variety of ways. Sometimes He is so clear that it actually takes effort to misunderstand Him, and at other times, He will deliberately veil His intended meaning.

The Law, for the most part, is very much on the cut and dry side of the equation. It is difficult to misunderstand Exodus 20:13, which clearly says, "You shall not murder" (NIV). Elsewhere in the Law, it even offers its own commentary about special, mitigating circumstances. For instance, "If a thief is caught while breaking in and is struck so that he dies, there will be no bloodguiltiness on his account. But if the sun has risen on him, there will be bloodguiltiness on his account" (Exod. 22:2–3). If you think about it for a moment, this makes sense. At night, it's hard to see; if you come upon a thief in the darkness in your home, it is reasonable that you shouldn't have to risk your life, the lives of those dwelling in your home, and your property just to protect him. In the daytime, however, there is ample light. You should be able to tell whether or not he is armed and deal appropriately with him without killing him. We could go onward and analyze other portions of the Law, but you get the idea. The Law is not supposed to be a mystery.

> "For this commandment which I command you today is not too difficult for you, nor is it out of reach. "It is not in heaven, that you should say, 'Who will go up to heaven for us to get it for us and make us hear it, that we may observe it?' Nor is it beyond the sea, that you should say, 'Who will cross the sea for us to get it for us and make us hear it, that we may observe it?' But the word is very near you, in your mouth and in your heart, that you may observe it."
>
> —DEUTERONOMY 30:11–14

On other occasions, the Lord will deliberately be less than clear.

> Hear now My words: If there is a prophet among you, I, the LORD, shall make Myself known to him in a vision I shall speak with him in a dream. Not so, with My servant Moses, He is faithful in all My household; With him I speak mouth to mouth, Even openly, and not in dark sayings.
>
> —NUMBERS 12:6–8

This is really an astounding statement. God is saying that the clarity He gave Moses was the exception to the rule, at least under the old covenant. With prophets, the Lord was saying that He would normally speak to them in dreams, visions, and dark sayings.[2] When reading the prophetic writings of the Old Testament, we need to take this deliberate obscurity into account.

When He does choose to obscure His meaning, the Lord frequently draws unexpected comparisons and analogies. This has two main purposes. First, He can say something in the hearing of everyone and only His intended audience will grasp His meaning. The Lord likes to have people who will choose to seek after Him. Generally, His intended audience includes only those who really want to know what He is saying; that's why the authors of Proverbs tell us to seek wisdom and to "incline" our "heart to understanding" (Prov. 2:2–5). They also say that "the fear of the LORD is the beginning of wisdom" (Prov. 9:10). If we fear Him, we will certainly want to know what He says.

The second purpose has to do with the volume of information. It is said that a picture paints a thousand words. Analogies have a way of painting pictures in our minds. If we take a little bit of time to look at them, it is amazing just how much they can say.

The Lord first started detailing the start of the war to the prophet Isaiah through one of these unexpected compari-

---

2 We who are under a better covenant need to expect more clarity than what the old covenant prophets often lived with: "No longer do I call you slaves, for the slave does not know what his master is doing; but I have called you friends, for all things that I have heard from My Father I have made known to you" (John 15:15).

sons. In Isaiah 14, the Lord starts talking about a nation called Babylon, who at the time is still small and insignificant and far away. He goes on to say that this nation will become very powerful and will subdue many other cities and nations. Babylon will even be the Lord's chosen instrument to bring judgment on His own rebellious people living in the land of Judea, but their reign of terror will not be eternal, because eventually He will bring them down.

Then the Lord starts focusing in on the king of Babylon, saying that the peoples of the world will celebrate his destruction and that the land will have rest in his absence. Then the Lord's discourse takes a turn for the macabre as he starts describing this "dearly" departed king's exit from this world and his arrival in the next.

> The grave below is all astir to meet you at your coming; it rouses the spirits of the departed to greet you—all those who were leaders in the world; it makes them rise from their thrones—all those who were kings over the nations. They will all respond, they will say to you, "You also have become weak, as we are; you have become like us." All your pomp has been brought down to the grave, along with the noise of your harps; maggots are spread out beneath you and worms cover you. How you have fallen from heaven, O morning star, son of the dawn!
> —ISAIAH 14:9–12

Depending on your translation it may say "Lucifer," instead of "morning star." If you pronounce the Hebrew word, it sounds like Lucifer. If you translate its meaning, you get "morning star." When the translators use "Lucifer" (the sound of the Hebrew word) instead of "morning star" (its meaning), we say they transliterated the word rather than translating it. Had I been in Isaiah's position and I didn't have to deal with the difference between translating and transliterating a word, I would have been a little confused. Son of the Dawn would have been a title of honor, especially coming from the Lord. To get such a title, the king of Babylon would have had to have been walking righteously at some point in his life, and we see no hint of him ever having such a walk anywhere in the Scriptures. Fast forward a couple thousand years, and we realize that the passage is really drawing a comparison between the king of Babylon and a fallen angel named Lucifer.

This is the first and only time that Lucifer is called by that name. It is also the first of only two passages in the Old Testament that really talk about the origins of the one we more commonly call Satan. His identity was not really important to those under the old covenant, because they were not called to directly contend with him. To this day the Jewish people see him as a somewhat unwilling servant of the Lord, not as an adversary that they are to contend with.

Picking up where we left off in the passage:

> How you have fallen from heaven, O morning star, son of the dawn! You have been cast down to the earth, you who once laid low the nations! You said in your heart, "I will ascend to heaven; I will raise my throne above the stars of God; I will sit enthroned on

the mount of assembly, on the utmost heights of the sacred mountain. I will ascend above the tops of the clouds; I will make myself like the Most High." But you are brought down to the grave, to the depths of the pit. Those who see you stare at you, they ponder your fate: "Is this the man who shook the earth and made kingdoms tremble?"

—Isaiah 14:12–17, niv

In these verses, the Lord compares Lucifer to an earthly king. They both became arrogant and wanted to set themselves up as God to rule over all creation. Jesus would later say that He saw Lucifer "fall like lightning from heaven" (Luke 10:18, niv). In other words, Lucifer no longer held an exalted office in heaven. He became unable to occupy his old place and position with the Lord; he fell. Revelation 12:4 also says that he took one third of the Lord's angels with him. Because Lucifer and these angels lost their position and citizenship in heaven, they moved the basis of their operation to Earth, even though they are still given access to the realm of heaven. In the Book of Job, Lucifer appears twice before the Lord. The Lord asks him where he has been spending his time, and Satan responds, "Roaming through the earth and going back and forth in it" (Job 1:7, niv).

From the time of his fall onward, he is not called Lucifer again. He is known only as Satan. Keep in mind that Lucifer and Satan are transliterations. *Lucifer* is the Hebrew word translated as "morning star" in the English language, while *Satan* is the Hebrew word translated as "adversary." What a demotion; he went from being called Morning Star (the ancient name for the planet Venus, the brightest object in the night sky next to the moon) to just being called the Adversary, the guy who is against the Lord. I think it's comical that although he is in total rebellion, his identity is still wrapped up in the Lord. Anytime Satan wants to talk about who he is, he ends up mentioning the Lord, whom he hates. Anytime he wants to talk about his mission, he ends up talking about the Lord. Everything he does is in reaction against the Lord; it may not be positive, but he still can't help talking about Him all the time.

The next critical event in the passage is where Satan is cast down to the earth. This is a future event, in which Satan's ability to move freely about in the spiritual realm will be completely taken from him and he will become a prisoner on the earth.[3] Revelation 12:7–14 talks about there being a war in heaven between the Lord's angels and Satan. The upshot of that war is that Satan is kicked out of (i.e., cast down from) all of heaven completely. We are embroiled in that "war" right now. (The Epilogue will cover what happens directly after this war is over.)

In America, we tend to think of a war roughly as two equal parties openly fighting each other. The war we are

---

3 Many people and commentators believe that Satan's fall and casting down, mentioned by Isaiah, are one and the same event. Revelation 12 talks about a war in heaven that results in Satan's being cast down to Earth. Verse 11 says that a particular group of people have a part to play using the blood of the Lamb and the word of their testimony. That group of people can't be anyone other than the redeemed church. They take the battle so seriously that the verse goes on to say that they "loved not their lives unto the death" (KJV). The following verses talk about Satan's response, which involves a number of events that have obviously not happened yet. Therefore, I conclude that Satan's complete casting down has not happened yet and that the church has a major part to play.

talking about is more of a rebellion that has exploded into open fighting between two parties who, as we shall see in later chapters, are anything but equally matched. In time, final victory will manifest in the favor of the Lord and His armies, as the rebellion is put down for all time.

Eventually, once the war and its aftermath are over, we will look down on Satan in astonishment, saying, "Is this the man who shook the earth and made kingdoms tremble?" (Isa. 14:16). Then he will go off to his fate of eternal judgment in the lake of fire, and we will never see him again.

Chapter 3

WHEN ANGELS FALL

A Good Thing Gone Wrong, Terribly Wrong

THIS IS ONE OF THOSE CHAPTERS THAT I HOPE YOU never have the misfortune of relating to. What has come out of the experiences that I will share with you is the thin silver lining around some of the darkest storm clouds I have ever seen. I apologize in advance, because this is not a happy chapter. Happy chapters come later, but now we need to revisit a tragedy.

In less than a year's time I had four of my closest friends walk away from the Lord. I remember the friendships we all had. I remember nights up late talking about the things of God or interceding for those around us. I remember times when we would pray together and the presence of the Lord would be so thick that unusual acts of God couldn't help but manifest. I knew two of them before they ever even accepted the Lord. I remember watching the daily transformations of new babes in Christ as they made so many wonderful discoveries about the Lord for the first time. Their new faith was a blessing to me and a reminder not to be so jaded about the world and the problems it contains. For that matter, it was a reminder not to be so frustrated with the church and the problems it contains as well.

And then, one by one, they abandoned the faith. I watched as the light of Christ in their eyes became darker. I listened as the innocence and joy in their voices turned to calloused sarcasm or just open bitterness. I remember the pain and frustration of feeling helpless to stop the horror that was unfolding before my eyes. As they distanced themselves from the Lord, their attitudes and outlooks on life changed.

Every gift that the Lord had given them stayed with them; after all, "the gifts and the calling of God are irrevocable" (Rom. 11:29). One of my friends had an amazing ability to discern what was happening around him. When he walked away from the Lord he started using his gift to discern which people were praying for him to return to the Lord; he would confront them with a line-by-line quote of what they had prayed and then discourage them with his refusal to return. Another friend of mine had a shocking ability to win friends and influence people. When she walked away, she immediately had a number of people around her who encouraged her in her new path. For a while, even the believers who didn't know her very well took her side, not realizing that she was actually walking away from the faith.

To this day I wonder if I somehow contributed to their decisions. Not one of them wants to speak to me. But, then, what would there be to talk about? Our friendships were entirely based on the Lord. I still miss every one of them terribly.

For several years I carried a lot of guilt over their decisions. Eventually I became willing to see that I had to lay it all down and move on. When I finally made that decision, our Father was so ready to bring healing to my hurting heart. Yet, I wonder who comforts Him. As hard as what I endured was, I can't imagine what the Lord went through during that time. They were my friends, but they were and still are His children. Now that I have two children of my own, I would like to think that I can relate, given all the love my heart holds for them, but no. I can't even conceive of it. No matter how much my heart expands, it will never be comparable to that of the Infinite One.

The really sad part is that our heavenly Father has been losing children almost every day for thousands of years. We usually go back to Adam and Eve when we talk of such things, but I want to go a little further back. I don't know if He looks on His angels as His children, but I know He cares for them. It was His most beautiful one who first turned. If you would like to get a piece of the Lord's heart, pay close attention to the first line of the following scripture. The Lord says, "Take up a lamentation," not a celebration. He is about to bring righteousness to the earth by way of judgment, and He says we should be weeping, not rejoicing.

> "Son of man, take up a lament concerning the king of Tyre and say to him: 'This is what the Sovereign LORD says: "'You were the model of perfection, full of wisdom and perfect in beauty. You were in Eden, the garden of God; every precious stone adorned you: ruby, topaz and emerald, chrysolite, onyx and jasper, sapphire, turquoise and beryl. Your settings

and mountings were made of gold; on the day you were created they were prepared. You were anointed as a guardian cherub, for so I ordained you. You were on the holy mount of God; you walked among the fiery stones. You were blameless in your ways from the day you were created till wickedness was found in you. Through your widespread trade you were filled with violence, and you sinned. So I drove you in disgrace from the mount of God, and I expelled you, O guardian cherub, from among the fiery stones. Your heart became proud on account of your beauty, and you corrupted your wisdom because of your splendor. So I threw you to the earth; I made a spectacle of you before kings. By your many sins and dishonest trade you have desecrated your sanctuaries. So I made a fire come out from you, and it consumed you, and I reduced you to ashes on the ground in the sight of all who were watching. All the nations who knew you are appalled at you; you have come to a horrible end and will be no more.'"

—EZEKIEL 28:12–19, NIV

If you remember from the last chapter, I said that there are two passages of scripture that plainly talk about our adversary's beginnings. This was the second one. Like the first, it compares Satan with an earthly king. The Isaiah passage mainly talks about the major transitions and events in Satan's life: he was created, he was corrupted, he fell, he will be cast down completely, and then He will be judged. This passage, from Ezekiel, talks mainly about who he was before he fell and how he fell.

My friends are not the people they used to be, and though they don't realize it, their perspectives have become distorted. (How else can you explain walking away from a perfect, loving Father?) They still have their original callings and gifts, but by misusing those gifts they can be very destructive. Because I knew them before they fell, I have some idea of their capabilities and possibly their potential weaknesses. If our struggle were against flesh and blood, this could be vital knowledge. Thankfully, it's not, so I am not in the position of having to fight against my friends.

The silver lining has two major parts for me. The first is that I have seen firsthand how rebellion takes the perfect creation of God and weakens and distorts it. I can to some extent use the information about Satan before his fall to understand some of his abilities and motivations now. The second is that my friends are still alive, which means that there is still time to pray for them, and there is still time for them to return to the Lord. If, like me, you have seen loved ones walk away from the Lord, take heart. As long as they draw breath, we can pray that the Lord will break through their shame, disappointment, offense, and whatever else keeps them from embracing the Lord. I look forward to the day when my friends come home to Jesus.

Going back to the first part of the silver lining, we know that Satan is a weakened, spiteful version of his former self. If we want to know what his capabilities are today, we need only to look at what he was designed to be able to do. So, in this chapter we are going to study him as he was.

In both the Ezekiel and the Isaiah passages, Satan is compared with a king. In those days, a king was responsible for his entire kingdom; he didn't answer to anyone but himself and God almighty. We think of the president of the United States as being in a position of power, but even he has to deal with the decisions of Congress and must abide by the judicial branch's interpretation of the laws of the land. If that isn't enough, after a mere four years, he has to face reelection by the majority vote of the U.S. populace. At best, he gets eight years to lead, because according to U.S. law he can't be reelected for a third four-year term. In ancient times, a king was a king, and his power was virtually absolute within the borders of his kingdom. History is filled with examples of kings whose political power went to their heads, and they proclaimed themselves gods in their own right.

Lucifer was originally designed to carry immense power, authority, and responsibility. Bear in mind that the kingdom of heaven was, is, and always will be the largest, most magnificent kingdom ever created. Lucifer was designed to administer a good portion of that kingdom on a day-to-day basis. Make no mistake, Satan is a talented leader. The potentially scary thing is that he has approximately one-third of the angelic populace of heaven at his disposal (Rev. 12:4). The full magnitude of the seriousness of this deserves some respect. One of heaven's most talented leaders has a third of heaven's army, and that leader is out to thwart God's plans in the earth by any means necessary—and we are in the middle of those plans. This is serious, but this is not a reason to fear. God is stronger, God is wiser, and most importantly, God is for us and not against us. Oh, and before I forget to mention it, God has an incredible plan. But more about that later. For now just remember that the end of the book has already been written, and it says we win. That's a rough translation, I know, but that's what it says (Rev. 20–22).

Ezekiel 28:12 says that he "had the seal of perfection." That is to say that he was a completed, perfect creation. Basically, God looked at him one day and said, "This is it, Lucifer. I'm finished creating you. Enjoy life as My greatest masterpiece thus far." Verses 12 through 15 describe what that completed work was like. He was "full of wisdom" (v. 12). I usually describe wisdom as having and using the knowledge and abilities God has given you to do things the best possible way. Being full of wisdom requires having tremendous knowledge, applying oneself to gain more knowledge, being observant, displaying diligence in all things, and walking uprightly. Now, Proverbs says, "The fear of the LORD is the beginning of wisdom" (Prov. 1:7). Satan has clearly lost the fear of the Lord and his upright nature, but the other capabilities that went along with his immense knowledge base and intelligence are still very much at his disposal.

As part of his perfection, the Lord said that he was "perfect in beauty" (v. 12). *Perfect* in this instance means "complete." So he was completely beautiful. The Lord went on to say that he wore a covering of precious stones, and He rattled off this most unusual list of stones, appearing in groups of threes: ruby, topaz, diamond; beryl, onyx, jasper; and lapis lazuli, turquoise, and emerald. I'll confess, for most of my life when I would read this passage of Scripture, my only thought was, "Wow, that must have been pretty—all those sparklies in one place." When I really stopped to think about it, my usual response would be a rather fleshly request made to the Lord: "Can I have one of those coverings when I get to heaven? I'd like to hang it over the mantle or something."

One day not too many years ago, the Lord had me researching the different precious and semiprecious stones in Scripture. One of my first discoveries was that I found another place where this exact list of stones occurs, in this order and in groups of threes. We see it on the breastplate worn by the high priest of Israel. The association of the high priest of Israel and the devil in the mind of God has several implications, some of them very good and some of them very bad. The Lord designed Lucifer in a very peculiar way, and He did it on purpose. It was no accident that he had those stones in his clothes. Sometime later when God instituted a high priesthood for Israel, there was a reason He had them pattern part of the high priest's uniform after part of Satan's old uniform.

The correlation stretches even further than stones. Lucifer also had settings and sockets of gold.

> You shall make a breastpiece of judgment, the work of a skillful workman; like the work of the ephod you shall make it: of gold, of blue and purple and scarlet material and fine twisted linen you shall make it. It shall be square and folded double, a span in length and a span in width. You shall mount on it four rows of stones; the first row shall be a row of ruby, topaz and emerald; and the second row a turquoise, a sapphire and a diamond; and the third row a jacinth, an agate and an amethyst; and the

fourth row a beryl and an onyx and a jasper; they shall be set in gold filigree.... You shall make on the breastpiece chains of twisted cordage work in pure gold. You shall make on the breastpiece two rings of gold, and shall put the two rings on the two ends of the breastpiece. You shall put the two cords of gold on the two rings at the ends of the breastpiece.

—EXODUS 28:15–20, 22–24

The only difference between what we know of Satan's covering and the breastplate is that the breastplate has one more set of three stones. The passage in Ezekiel says that "every precious stone was your covering" (Ezek. 28:13), it is probable that the list we are given is only a partial one. I take this to mean that Satan was the original high priest.

The correlation goes beyond the uniform. He was "the anointed cherub" (Ezek. 28:14). There are only two general positions that are described as "anointed" in the Old Testament. The first is the priest. All priests had to be anointed in order to serve (Exod. 30:30; Lev. 4:3, 5, 16). The second is the king (1 Sam. 10:1; 2 Sam. 1:14). In this passage the Lord is choosing to compare Satan with both positions.

At first glance, one has to wonder what a priest was good for in heaven. A priest is an intermediary. They are the original intercessors. A priest's job is to represent God to the people and to represent the people before the Lord. In Protestant churches we sometimes have an unnecessarily poor view of priests. We are prone to think that the new covenant through the remission of our sins has abolished the office of the priest, and that where they do exist they end up getting in the way of our being able to go directly before the Lord. This is a gross misunderstanding of the priestly function that comes from not reading the old covenant very carefully. Priests were instituted to minister before the Lord and to help others worship and serve the Lord. During the time covered under the old covenant, sin reigned in the earth, which made approaching God a dangerous business. A sinful human and a Holy God just don't mix. So in order for people to safely approach God, that sin had to be covered over (atoned for). The priests ended up spending a great deal of time making sure that their own sin was covered; then, in order to take others into the presence of the Lord, they would help others get their sins covered. Only after all the sin was taken care of could the real worshiping and interacting with the Lord begin.

Jesus came along and removed the sin issue, which removed the greatest obstacle to mankind experiencing a relationship with God. He opened the way for a real life with God to happen. He also made us all priests under Himself, the great High Priest. In addition to ministering before and worshiping the Lord, we are called to minister one to another. For instance, we pray for and with each other. In a similar way, Lucifer was the primary agent to help the other angels interact with the Lord.

One of the ways that he helped was that he "covered." I believe that Lucifer was designed to protect others from the presence of God. God's presence, when it manifests in full-ness, is a dangerous thing (Ps. 97:5). By covering others, Lucifer could escort them much closer to the throne. Today he uses that same ability to cast a pall over the spiritual senses of the whole earth. He does his very best to separate us from experiencing the Father. To some extent, most demons do a little of this. Countless times I have physically felt the presence of demons. I have had several occasions where I could feel the presence of the Lord in the air around me, and then a demon walked into the room and chilled the spiritual climate a good 40 degrees. At those times I usually reach inside to continue contact with the Lord. A demon can sometimes interrupt an external manifestation of the Lord, but taking away the Lord who dwells in us is not within the scope of their abilities.

Satan currently uses all of his knowledge and abilities as a former high priest to function as a sort of anti-priest. He does everything he can to prevent us from experiencing a living, thriving relationship with the Father; then he promotes every form of idolatry imaginable. How Satan accomplishes his goals is the subject of Part II in this book. Here I just want you to see that he was designed to help people worship God and that now he uses his expertise to prevent people from worshiping God. He desires for them to worship something—anything—else instead.

His position as high priest almost certainly gave him access to and the respect of every angel in heaven. I'd be willing to bet that he used that position to his advantage when he enticed one-third of God's angels to rebel. Even with the position and prestige that he enjoyed, he still had to be an incredible tempter to convince such a large number of angels, who could see God so plainly, to turn against Him.

So let's sum this up into one picture: Satan is a very talented leader and administrator, who has command over a very large number of fallen angels. He is extremely intelligent and knowledgeable and can argue very convincingly. As heaven's former high priest, he knows how to interact with the Lord, so to a large extent he knows what we should be doing. He also uses everything he knows about worship to render mankind's efforts ineffective and to encourage mankind to focus on anything but the Lord.

This is not a pretty picture. Thankfully, we have an even more impressive Leader on our side, and He has a truly amazing plan.

Chapter 4

THE LORD'S RESPONSE

I T WAS A SAD DAY IN HEAVEN WHEN LUCIFER FELL. Many of heaven's finest had been corrupted and summarily kicked out. I can imagine standing inside the city watching a seemingly endless river of blackness flow out of the pearl gates. I watch in sadness as the putrid cloud moves through space in the lower heavens and exits in outer space, just over a beautiful, blue-green sphere. I can see the enraged storm descend on the unprotected earth, where they will have free reign to vent the fury they feel over their great loss. The rebellion had failed; heaven would not become Satan's personal property, but earth was ripe for the picking.

With nothing to stand in their way, I imagine it didn't take long for Earth to be stripped bare of virtually all life. So with heaven impervious to attack and Earth now unoccupied except for the demons, the war came to a standstill. All awaited God's next move. Would He invade Earth with an army of angels? Would He wipe it off the map? No, there would be no glory in either of those options. Satan would be able to boast that he created a mess so corrupt that God could bring no good from it; thus, he could boast that in some way He was more powerful than God. No, God wasn't through with Satan or with the earth.

In the coming millennia, Satan would discover that God is capable of a truly amazing, totally unexpected feat—redemption. Really, the whole war centers around the question, Is there anything God can't redeem? To start the process, God would allow Satan to go as far as he was capable in destroying the earth. Satan didn't realize that by sweeping the earth bare, he was leaving God with a clean slate.

Then the Holy Spirit descended, moving over the waters of the deep, and He spoke:

> Let there be light.... Let the waters under the heaven be gathered together unto one place, and let dry land appear.
> —GENESIS 1:3, 9, KJV

> Let the earth sprout vegetation.
> —GENESIS 1:11

Helpless to stop the mighty hand of God, the demons just watched and cursed, "We'll just destroy this one like the last one." Then day six arrived, and God did something unexpected.

> Let us make man in Our image, according to Our likeness; and let them rule over....
> —GENESIS 1:26

"Man?" the demons hissed. "What's a man? And it's supposed to rule over everything on Earth?"

The demons got the shock of the millennium when they first saw Adam. Here was a creature unlike anything they had ever seen. He looked just like God, only he was contained in flesh, and God gave him the deed to the earth. Suddenly the demons' home wasn't theirs anymore. If they wanted to do something, then they would need permission. This was not good. Since no one had any ideas as to what to do yet, they waited and watched.

Since Adam would need food and a place to stay, God planted a garden and charged Adam with cultivating and protecting it (Gen. 2:15). Partly to help Adam familiarize himself with his kingdom and partly for a loving Father's amusement, God brought each of the world's animals before him so that Adam could pick names for them. Then God gave Adam a commandment: "Eat from any tree you want, except that one in the middle over there" (Gen. 2:17, author's paraphrase). The tree of the knowledge of good and evil wasn't hard to recognize. It looked like the only thing that didn't belong in so serene a place; it was eerily exotic. I imagine it was also the only thing in the garden that didn't have the tangible presence of God on it. Who would want to eat that?

Seeing that Adam had gotten comfortable enough in the garden to realize that he was alone, the Lord decided that it was time to make a companion for him. So He put Adam to sleep for a while, and when he awoke he could feel that he was missing a rib. After his eyes adjusted to the light of day around him, they began to focus on a creature more exquisitely beautiful than any animal he had seen. That must be her. He would call her "woman," because she came out of him.

Looking on from a distance, the demons were surely

bemoaning their current predicament. One of these man-creatures was bad enough, but now there were two of them. It wouldn't be long before God told them of the presence of demons on their planet, and it would be all over. Even if He didn't bother to mention that there were demons to remove, these creatures obviously had the ability to reproduce; they would soon fill the earth anyway. Having been outside of the upper heavens for so long, they had gotten accustomed to a place that reflected their nature. These two humans were anything but demonic. In reality, they contained more of the substance of God than any angel ever had. Let them increase in number, and conditions on Earth would become completely intolerable. Something had to be done.

Where all of hell's number must have seen a threat, Satan saw an opportunity. He had been in this place before. He was grossly outnumbered at the start of his rebellion. He had started by isolating and influencing the most weak-minded angels. As they began to see things his way, they would continue the work for him. As his ranks grew, his rebellion began to take on a momentum and life of its own. Eventually, every angel in heaven had to choose a side. Too bad for him, he only managed to corrupt one in three. Having had some practice at this, he knew what he was doing this time; he would start with the one who was obviously the most unprepared for the encounter.

A few days later, Eve was in the center of the garden, and Adam was introducing her to the different creatures. So, seizing the opportunity, Satan concealed himself as a natural serpent and started a conversation with Eve. His plan went off without a hitch. Eve was totally unprepared for their conversation. The only thing she knew was that God said not to eat the fruit from the tree of the knowledge of good and evil. She did not know what evil was, much less that she needed to be able to combat it. Satan suggested that God told her not to eat the fruit because it would make her like Him. The implication: God was holding out on her by trying to prevent her from being all that she could be. Since no one present told her differently, she naively listened to the snake.

Now, Adam was in love with Eve and would have followed her anywhere. When Eve went to share her wonderful new food with him, he ate it without thinking.

Immediately, they became naked. They had never worn clothes in the natural because they lived under the Lord's love and were clothed with His glory. When they had both eaten, the glory lifted and shame set in. They found themselves needing something. Being unable to settle a deep, spiritual need through spiritual means, they had to compensate in the natural. So they hid and went looking for fig leaves to cover themselves. At best this was akin to using a Band-Aid to cover a gaping, mortal wound.

When Satan's angels fell, they immediately went from being totally for God to totally, hopelessly against Him. This is because they were designed with a relatively simple nature; they were created to fulfill various functions. In Scripture, we see them as watchers, covering cherubs, and ministering spirits, among other roles (Dan. 4:17; Ezek. 28:16; Heb. 1:14). They are servants. They will either serve God totally, or they will completely side against Him and serve something else.

Man was not made to be a servant only. Man was created in the image of God for the purpose of relationship. Once the glory departed and sin set in, it would corrupt him by degrees. In any event, the nature of man was now flawed. When a child is born he is innocent, but he is in possession of a flawed nature. As a man lives, he inadvertently sins more and more, driving the expression of that flaw throughout his being; eventually his mind considers evil only. It is for this reason that the Lord mercifully shortened the days of man from surviving as long as an oak tree to somewhere between eighty and one hundred and twenty years.

To show the humans that their sin had changed them and not Him, God kept to His regular routine with them. Toward the end of the day God appeared in the garden and called to them. Once they admitted to being naked, He began to address what had happened.

First, He turned to Adam, the one who absolutely knew better, for an explanation. He was giving Adam a chance to own up to his sin and to have a part in putting it right. If Adam would have said, "Lord, it's all my fault." He would, in essence, have been taking his proper authority over the whole situation and representing both himself and his wife before the Lord. It would have been a very priestly thing for him to do. Adam gave up his chance and, with it, the authority over that defining moment when he passed the buck to Eve.

Eve was now mankind's last hope for several thousand years. Unfortunately, she didn't do any better than her husband. Eve passed the chance on to the snake.

Satan knew that he would bear the brunt of the Lord's righteous indignation for the situation if he couldn't (or wouldn't) find someplace else to put the blame. But that indignation was a small price to pay to possess a great deal of mankind's authority.

Then God began to explain the consequences of their sin. For Adam, his arena was tending the garden and, by extension, all the land on earth. As a natural consequence, the effects of sin entered into everything he would put his hand to, which included the land. Eve had been called to bring forth new life in the earth. Because she had death reigning in her mortal body, bringing forth life—the opposite of death— would require a struggle.

As for Satan, he had nothing to lose and everything to gain. Because he had sinned through his rebellion, he had already experienced the consequences of his sin. He had lost his place, position, and identity in heaven with the Lord. Taking on the sin of man did not demote him any further. However, by taking responsibility for it, he gained authority over man concerning this issue. He wanted a place, position, and identity in the earth from which he could rule. This is what he gained when he agreed to be accountable for sin. Therefore, God began to pronounce judgment against him and his role in his new position. Satan was originally a cherub, an order of angel that in every description in Scripture has both legs and wings; he would lose both. Furthermore, he would be at war with mankind and would eventually be defeated by one particular man at great personal cost to himself.

Last chapter I said that Satan was once God's high priest and that this had considerable implications, both good and bad. The bad implications showed up most clearly before the time of Jesus. When God looked to Adam to explain what happened, He was wanting Adam to act as a priest would. In other words, He wanted Adam to intercede for his wife and himself. But Adam ceded his authority to Eve, who gave it away to Satan. This time around sin was in the equation, and Satan used that sin as a means to accuse mankind before the throne of God day and night (Rev. 12:10). He also used his expertise as a high priest to set up idolatrous religions so that people, in effect, were worshiping him and other demonic members of his army.

Were it not for that prophecy about mankind getting a savior, Satan would have stood there in the garden gloating for a much longer time. For the next four thousand or so years, Satan would use his newfound authority to enslave mankind within an existence far beneath what the Lord had desired for them. It was no coincidence that every time God's people started crying out for deliverance, children started being murdered in mass. Satan was trying to prevent that Savior from coming forth.

For four thousand years, Satan nervously waited for his chance to strike at the one who would be his undoing. Then, in the tiny village of Bethlehem, God did something even Satan did not expect; God sent Himself. Contending with God personally was not Satan's idea of a good time, nor was it on his agenda. Satan was expecting a man, another David or Samson or Samuel, someone who could be reasoned with and tempted. He was not expecting God to personally step off His throne, put on the limitations of human flesh, and step into the middle of the struggle.

In fairness, the Lord gave Satan a specific chance to tempt Him. We all know the outcome of that encounter. For the first time since the garden, a man walked around not in sin and therefore not under the dominion of Satan, and for three and one-half years He walked all over the devil.

I suspect that the devil thought that God's plan was for mankind to join Jesus in life. He would heal all of their diseases and teach them a better way to live. They would learn to obey Him in all things. It would be an earthly kingdom run by Jesus Himself. Oh, how he so underestimated the Lord.

God's plan was to pick up where Adam left off. To stop the flow of sin in the world, He was going to take the penalty Adam should have volunteered for. The only problem with that logic is that Satan was in charge now. He was (thank you, Adam) the acting arbitrator between God and man. If someone was going to die for the sin of the world, Satan would have to be involved in that killing. Given the way that Satan saw things playing out, crucifying Christ prevented Him from setting up His earthly kingdom and personally ruling from Jerusalem. Killing Jesus was therefore Satan's best option; too bad for him, it was exactly what the Lord wanted.

> We speak of God's wisdom in a mystery...the wisdom which none of the rulers of this age understood; for if they had understood it, they would not have crucified the Lord of glory.
> —1 CORINTHIANS 2:7–8

To get a few things theologically straight: if Adam had tried to accept responsibility, it would not have automatically cleared us of our sin problem. Sin, when it exists, will kill someone. Adam was already dead from the moment he swallowed the first bite of the fruit from that awful tree. He couldn't give his life because he didn't have it anymore. What would have happened is that Satan would never have obtained Adam's authority. Also, it's possible that God might have sped up the redemptive work, because Adam would have been in a place to partner with Him. As it was, God had to wait several thousand years until He could trick the devil into partnering with Him in His redemptive plan. It was a brilliant ruse, timed perfectly; and Satan fell for it hook, line, and sinker.

Once Satan gave Christ the just penalty for the sins of the world, Jesus reclaimed the authority and position that originally belonged to Adam. In addition, as a reward for His suffering, God the Father gave Christ the position and title of King of kings and Lord of lords (Rev. 17:14). Unlike Satan, Jesus would use that position to pardon anyone who would come to Him. In one day, humanity gained a high priest so awesome He defies comprehension.

But wait; there's more. He gave us the right to become sons of God, coheirs with Himself, a royal priesthood. We have been freely given what Satan always wanted, equality with God. Now, before you stone me for blasphemy, let me explain. We were made in the image of God (Gen. 1:26). We are now part of a royal priesthood just under Christ, our great High Priest. Jesus even quoted Isaiah in saying that we are all gods (John 10:34–35). When any part of the Lord's creation looks at a redeemed person and compares us to Jesus, they don't see much difference, because we were made to be exactly like Him. We are still under Him, and He has more than earned our praise, worship, and adoration; indeed, He is the only one who should be worshiped. In order not to get arrogant and make Lucifer's mistake, we need to remember that our place with God is not based on our works but His. If any boasting is to be done, let it be in and because of Him and the great things He has done. If you want to put the book down, and run around, and celebrate and sing praises to the Lord (and do some good old fashion boasting in Him), this would be an appropriate time. Lord willing, this book will still be available when you are done.

I personally think this gets even more interesting when we consider our place in Christ in relation to the present war. Everything Lucifer used to have now belongs to Jesus, who willingly shares it with us. In addition to being children of God and all that entails, we, along with Christ, are also Lucifer's replacements. Think about it. Lucifer used to be the high priest, and his angels used to serve under him; now Jesus is the High Priest, and we are part of His royal priesthood (Matt. 16:19; John 17:22–23). Satan and his army are only imposters, whereas we are the real thing.

What really blows my mind is not the change in position with the Lord, but the change in our nature. Adam was created as a flawless human who was in harmony with the Lord. Adam was also given an eternal spirit (Gen. 2:7). When he sinned, his very nature became flawed, and mankind gained an irresistible tendency to sin (Rom. 3:10, 23). When we accept Christ, we exchange our old, flawed nature for His perfect, sinless nature (Rom. 6:6–8). Our real nature is now the nature of Christ, which now has a tendency to follow and obey the Father. Regarding issues of sin, we are now given a choice; we can put on the old man, or we can put off the old man and put on Christ (Col. 3:9–11). Satan's best temptations don't have to work on us any longer. We actually have a choice in the matter.

Because of the work of Christ, the devil is rendered positionless *and* weaponless. If you are struggling with a sin issue, the instruction for victory is very simple: "Walk by the spirit, and you will not carry out the desire of the flesh" (Gal. 5:16). In other words, get in God and live for Him all the time, and as a natural consequence you will not fulfill the desires of the flesh. All of Satan's best weapons won't be able to work on you.

Satan and his entire army should have been groveling at the feet of the church centuries ago. He has been able to maintain his current influence in the earth for one main reason: we, the church, let him. The good news is, the fat lady has not sung yet. The show is not over, and it won't end until after the church has been declared victorious. We have the option of seizing victory now in this generation or of putting it off until another generation should come along. I don't know about you, but given the choice, I choose now!

Chapter 5

THE TWISTED MIND
OF A DEMON

So, what are they thinking? They are out-manned, outgunned, and outmaneuvered. Satan managed to corrupt one-third of the Lord's angels—an accomplishment to be sure—but that leaves two-thirds still serving the Lord. Surely he is capable of doing the math, which says that for every one angel on his side there are two angels against him. To make matters worse, the Lord's angels are equipped with the arsenal of heaven, which includes flaming swords (Gen. 3), flaming chariots (2 Kings 6:17), and who knows what else. This doesn't even account for God's most powerful weapon, the redeemed church in union with Himself. As for being outmaneuvered, God knows every-thing. Can you imagine being up against an opponent who knows all of your plans centuries before you come up with them? With odds like that, what is the devil thinking? What can he possibly hope to accomplish? For that matter, why would his entire army consent to continue following him into a mission that is so obviously doomed to failure?

The answer is surprisingly simple: they're crazy. No, really.

They are totally and completely nuts! Referring to Satan, the Scriptures say, "He was a murderer from the beginning, not holding to the truth, for there is no truth in him. When he lies, he speaks his native language, for he is a liar and the father of lies" (John 8:44, NIV). I don't know about you, but growing up we acknowledged the devil but never thought about him too deeply or for too long; at most I only gave this verse a cursory reading, and the only things I drew from it were that he was both a murderer and the first liar. I thought of the statement, "Not holding to the truth, for there is no truth in him," as little more than poetic language. I have since learned that there are no wasted words when the Lord speaks. So, after repenting for my cherry-picking heart I began to take this verse more seriously. *The truth* is probably best defined as "the way things really are." If we want we can replace the word *truth* with *reality* in that verse and get, "Not holding to reality, for there is no reality in him." Satan does not and is not able to take things as they really are. He is completely out of touch with reality. He's crazy, and the really unnerving part is that he was not deceived by some third party. He willingly allowed himself to be corrupted by his own beauty and accomplishments.

Oddly enough, the nature of his insanity can be understood to some degree by the mind of man. This understanding can actually yield some of the most useful information in this book, because when you know the mind of your opponent you can predict their actions. To illustrate this point I have a couple of examples from my own life.

So, here I am again playing a game of chess with someone for the first time. This victim's name is Ralf. Did I say "victim"?

I meant opponent. Yeah, that's right—opponent. I love to play chess. Really, I love just about any game involving some level of strategy. I enjoy coming up with elegant solutions to the difficult problems people throw at me. The real fun is when I can turn their best plans against them and seemingly take victory with ease. But I digress. Today it's chess, and the *opponent's* name is Ralf. I've never played Ralf before, and I haven't seen him play anyone else; so, I'm not sure what to expect. What are his strengths? His weaknesses? At this point I don't know. I'll have to play him to find out.

Twenty-five moves and about as many minutes later I finally beat him. I played him in several games after that, and most of them were over in about half as many moves. My secret to success? I study and learn my opponents' strategies, strengths, and weaknesses. Then I adjust my strategies accordingly. I realized Ralf has no idea what he is doing with most of his pieces. Oh, he knows the rules of the game, and he can move his pieces around just fine. But, he only knows how to really exploit his queen and his bishops. In future games, I would focus a great deal of my efforts on neutralizing those pieces. The first game I play against an opponent is usually my worst. By the second or third game, they either come up with something new to throw at me, or I will beat them hands down. I have outwitted several players who are otherwise better than I am solely on this principle.

Now, I confess I overstated my ignorance of Ralf's chess game. Before we sat down to that game, I had been around him for weeks, so I knew an awful lot about his character and his approach to daily life. I knew that he tended to be highly reactive emotionally to the world around him. When he could look at something objectively, his observations and decision-making were perfectly fine. However, once his emotions got involved, he could become very irrational very quickly. I figured that as a chess player he would play the game in just as undisciplined a manner by choosing to make moves that looked and felt good on the surface, but when push came to shove he probably wouldn't be willing or able to study the board long enough to see three or four moves into the future. This meant that I could very easily lead Ralf into any trap I wanted. All I had to do was offer him a good-looking move (like a "free" piece), and he would go for it every time. My real ignorance with him before that first game was really a question of how good-looking the "good-looking" move had to be and how much I would have to disguise the threat to get him to fall for it. Once I had a feel for that, it worked every time. He inevitably failed to realize that by going after the "free" piece, he was leaving something else undefended.

After years of exploiting my knowledge of my adversaries in various board games against human opponents and in spiritual warfare against the demonic hordes, it still strikes me as odd that a person's character can be used to predict their strategies. Someone once told me a joke about the devil: "How do you know when the devil is lying? Answer: his lips are moving." Remember John 8:44; the devil is a liar. A liar is someone who intentionally deceives. He may admit to certain elements of the truth, but his intent is *always* to deceive, because that is what liars do. The odd part is that he couldn't tell the truth even if he wanted to, because "the truth is not in him." So, whenever a demon is trying to convince you of something, right away, you know that it's a lie. Demons can sound convincing because they believe their own hype, but trust me when I say they are still lying. I called this chapter "The Twisted Mind of a Demon" for precisely this reason; only a twisted mind could know that they are lying and yet believe the lie at the same time. Like I said, they're crazy.

Let's take an example: Say a demon is telling you that you are ugly and that because you are ugly you will never find a marriageable mate, because no one of the opposite sex would so much as look at you. Because a demon is the one talking, we know that *at least* one of those statements is false. It could be that you are very beautiful and you are just having trouble seeing it at the time; or maybe you are physically unattractive in the eyes of most people, but the Lord still has a mate picked out for you who will love you more than you can comprehend. Generally, the more emotionally painful a demon's statement is, the further it is from the truth. If the truth of the matter does not clearly jump out at you when you recognize that the devil is talking and therefore lying to you, just turn to your loving heavenly Father. Remember, the Lord is *not* a liar, and His Holy Spirit *will* lead and guide you into *all* truth. (Oh, and if you think you are ugly, I'd like to point out that in Christ you are a new creation, and the Lord doesn't make junk.)

I pray often for discernment to know who is speaking to me. I ask, Am I imagining things? Is some demon trying to bring confusion or doubt, or is the Lord trying to tell me something? Knowing who is talking makes all the difference.

Let's take the board game analogy a little further. If I sat down with Ralf over a game of Risk (another classic strategy game), I could make a pretty good guess as to how he would play based on his performance in our chess games. People have natural approaches to the world and to both its everyday and its extraordinary challenges. Generally their initial approach is roughly the same from one situation to another, this holds true no matter how good a strategist they are.

So what else is consistent about our adversary? Well, John 10:10 says that, "The thief comes only to steal and kill and destroy." His motivations are purely destructive. We can't reason with him. It is useless to make truces and treaties with him because he is a liar who desires to bring destruction; he will break them at his convenience. I have a policy of never negotiating or making agreements with the devil. Thankfully, Jesus has given us enough power and authority that we will never have to.

Also, if you know that the devil is active or interested in a situation, it usually isn't too hard to figure out what he is trying to accomplish. Simply ask what his capabilities are given the situation and how he could use them to "steal, kill, and destroy." Just don't forget to check your hypothesis with the Lord before you run with it. Remember, He has given us His Holy Spirit, who "will guide you into all the truth" (John 16:13). He does not want you to be confused or to believe the wrong thing.

I have another friend who is a much better strategist than Ralf; his name is Cid. In pretty much every game I have ever played with him, I found that he was a consistently good defensive player. If I wanted to take a piece from him in a game of chess, I knew I was going to have to earn it. On top of being a solid player he had one more surprise for me: he liked to talk. If you don't play strategy games or gamble, you may not have noticed this, but chess players and poker players have one thing in common: they don't talk. What's more, Cid uses his mouth as a method of distraction and confusion. He talks to his opponents about the game at hand and actually tries to trick them into making foolish mistakes. This worked on me for about three games. Then I noticed a pattern; the more trouble he was in, the more he talked. I began to use this as a barometer to know when I had found a move that he really didn't want me to make. Basically, I took what I knew of the devil in life and applied it to Cid as it relates to chess.

This knowledge of character works in reverse as well. Our adversary has been making observations of humanity for thousands of years. He has a knack for finding the weaknesses in our characters and exploiting them. He knows the lies that we are most likely to believe, and He will readily use them to lead us to all sorts of disasters. Many people are hesitant to engage in direct warfare with the enemy, because they don't want to be exposed to their deceptive schemes. Some people avoid spiritual encounters altogether for the same reason. Avoidance is the worst policy.

> The god of this world has blinded the minds of the unbelieving.
> —2 CORINTHIANS 4:4

Ignoring the devil will not make him go away. If anything, it just allows him to move more freely, because he is not being opposed. As followers of Christ, we need to stay as close to Jesus as possible and listen to the Holy Spirit constantly. That same Holy Spirit will lead and guide us into all truth, and He will help us in our weaknesses if we allow Him. By walking very closely with the Lord, you will, either directly or indirectly, end up confronting and overcoming the works of the devil in your life and the world around you.

I have one last piece of counsel. When you have encounters with our adversary, learn from them. Better yet, ask the Lord to teach you out of them so that you will be more prepared next time. By significant searching of the experience and through countless encounters with both the Lord and the devil, I have learned something: our enemy is a finite, predictable being. Our God is not.

> For as the heavens are higher than the earth, So are my ways higher than your ways And My thoughts than your thoughts.
> —ISAIAH 55:9

The one greatest variable between one battle and the next is the Lord's plan for victory. Stay close to Him so that you can be on page with Him at all times, because "apart from Me [Jesus] you can do nothing" (John 15:5) and "with God all things are possible" (Matt. 19:26).

Chapter 6

SATAN'S PIPE DREAM

THE SCENE STARTED IN HEAVEN. GOD, AN UNIMAGIN-ably bright being of such transcendent beauty and awesome power that just the sight of Him knocks people to their knees, was sitting on His throne made of jasper. Before Him, bright, shining angels assembled. By the millions upon millions they gathered until their number extended for miles in every direction upon the sea of crystal. Just as the assembly was being called to order, a hideous black, multi-headed, snake-like monster slithered up to the throne with an unmistakable air of pride and disrespect. Among such a glorious crowd, such a grotesque creature looked very out of place. Some of the angels whispered among each other, "What is *he* doing here? And why today of all days?" One of the watchers, an angel who spent most of his time by the throne of God, had seen this before; he quietly responded, "He is here to continue his latest argument with God, and he picked today because he wants everyone to see something." Just as they were about to ask what he was talking about, the conversation between the Lord and the devil started.

The Lord was the first to speak. "Where have you been?"

The angels close by the throne knew that their Master never asked a question because He didn't know the answer. Their musing about the Lord's intentions was interrupted as the creature spoke. "From roaming about on the earth, from here to there." Such an evasive answer; he was definitely up to something.

"Have you considered My servant Job? There is no one like him on Earth. He is blameless and upright. He fears God and turns from evil."

Apparently he had, because he knew exactly whom God was talking about—and so did all the angels present. Such a righteous man always has the attention of heaven.

Satan's response revealed a shocking condescension: "Have you not put a hedge of protection around him and all that he has? Have you not blessed all that he puts his hand to so that his possessions have become numberless? But strike what he has. Take everything from him, and he will curse you to your face."

"So that's it. He's questioning the Master's judgment of Job's character." The other angels looked back at the Watcher expecting more. He gestured for them to continue watching.

The Lord replied to Satan, "Go ahead. Take all he has; just don't hurt him."

As Satan confidently strode out, seven hissing heads held high, the other angels turned back to the Watcher. "He has been coming in and out of this place for centuries trying to argue with God."

"But why?"

"You all remember when he and the others fell." How could they forget it? One day they were talking to their friends, and then over the course of a few days their friends started questioning the Lord's right to rule and started talking about setting up their own kingdom. During that time, as their speech became more and more irrational, the light of God began to grow dimmer and dimmer in them. On the last day, as the light went out, their forms were hideously disfigured as they suddenly degenerated into awful, demonic maniacs. "That was the last time they tried to fight us in a pitched battle against the gates of heaven. Satan knows that he will never take the Almighty's throne by force. So, unable to rise to be God's equal, he has been trying to reduce the Holy One to his level. The only way to do that is to prove that the perfect God is deficient in some manner and therefore unfit to be the universal Judge and Lord of all. If that happens, then God is no longer justified in judging Satan for trying to set himself up as a god to be worshiped, and He can no longer rightly stand in his way."

The Watcher paused to let them consider his words. He could see the looks of shock and horror as they realized just how depraved their old friends had become. Just then, one of them asked the question the others had been thinking. "So what does this have to do with Job?"

"Satan thinks that God was unjustified in showing so much favor to Job. He thinks that God is playing favorites. If Job turns on God, then he will have inadvertently proven Satan correct." They all loved Job. His humility before and loyalty to the Lord were fast becoming legendary. But would he choose God after being handed over to Satan for no apparent reason?

Back on Earth, Satan found a sight he had been dreaming

about for months—Job, undefended. Satan took a few days to prepare his plan, and the only thing he sent Job's way was a sense of foreboding and the thought that the Lord might abandon him. Of course, with all Job had, he would reject those deceiving thoughts outright as being unreasonable. But what would happen when they got proven true in a sudden and frightening way? Suddenly they would sound like rational thinking, or so the devil thought.

On the appointed day and without warning, Satan struck. He killed all of Job's children, stole all of his livestock, and destroyed all of his crops. Only four of his servants survived, and the effect couldn't have gone more perfectly. One right after another, the survivors arrived to tell Job of the calamities that had befallen his household. "As soon as he gets over the initial shock, the fist shaking will begin," Satan said to himself as he watched with an air of triumph.

But what's this? Amid Satan's gloating, Job got up, tore his clothing, and began worshiping the Lord. "Naked I came from my mother's womb, and naked I shall return. The Lord gave and the Lord has taken away. Blessed be the name of the Lord."

The devil stood there stunned and quickly regained his composure. "That's all right. I'll give him some time. He'll wear out, and then he will behave just like everyone else." But Job didn't behave like everyone else. "Through all this Job did not sin nor did he blame God" (Job 1:22). It didn't take long to for Satan to realize that he would have to up the ante against Job's faithfulness; the next time he would request that he be allowed to hurt Job physically.

I won't bore you by writing out the rest of the story of

Job. We all know how it turns out, and you can read the full account in the Book of Job. Satan tormented Job by every method he could, short of actually killing him, and Job refused to denounce and accuse God. Eventually, God and Job had a conversation, and everything was restored to Job, with a double portion. The result was that Satan was proven wrong (again); thus, the Lord's assessment of Job's character was justified.

Satan is a talker. He will continue arguing with and accusing God until he is thrown into the lake of fire (Rev. 20:10). Satan's dream is to win an argument against God, and after six thousand years of human history, the Lord's winning streak is still unbroken. Yet the arguments extend further than words. There are several times in human history when the Lord has announced certain actions that He would perform (we call this prophecy); a few of those actions would and will only happen after certain other events line up. Satan spends a lot of energy in an effort to prevent those other events from coming to pass.

For instance, God promised that He would bless the whole world through the offspring of Abraham (Gen. 22:18). So, from the earliest times Satan has tried to kill off the Jewish people, because if there are no Jews there can be no widespread blessing through them. For example: there are several accounts through 1 and 2 Kings and 1 and 2 Chronicles of armies coming with the intent of destroying Israel and its populace, and in the time of Esther, Haman hatched a plot to annihilate all the Jews in the world.

Skip ahead a couple thousand years to the life of Jesus. On his last trip to Jerusalem, before the Jewish leaders conspired together to have Him crucified, Jesus upped the ante when He said, "Jerusalem, Jerusalem, who kills the prophets and stones those who are sent to her!...For I say to you, from now on you shall not see Me until you say, 'Blessed is He who comes in the name of the Lord!'" (Matt. 23:37, 39). If Satan can kill off all the Jews and then wipe Jerusalem off the map, then there won't be any Jews in Jerusalem to say, "Blessed is He who comes in the name of the Lord." At a minimum, that means that Jesus would never return to Earth and set up His kingdom in Jerusalem. Not surprisingly, from that day onward anti-Semitism took on a whole new fervor, in part because it is in the devil's best interest to kill off the Jews.

Satan wants nothing more than to prove God a liar who does not fulfill His promises. If Satan ever succeeds, then God will no longer be justified in judging him. At that point, Satan can argue that he's actually more morally upstanding than God, because at least he hasn't been hiding his true nature for all eternity past.

On a more personal note, you can bet that whenever God speaks a promise to you, some demon will show up to oppose it. The only advice I have for the believer in this situation is to stand firm and not doubt God or His promises to us (Eph. 6:10–18). Remember that God's promises are irrevocable.

PART II

Chapter 7

AUTHORITY, PART 1

THE CORNERSTONE OF SPIRITUAL WARFARE IS authority. Nothing happens without it. Earlier I said that Satan stole or, rather, tricked man into giving up his authority as a priest before the Lord. As we know, Jesus was sent many years later to restore that authority to the Lord's people, and now we can all walk in it.

The authority that Satan acquired in the Garden of Eden was only half the picture. The Lord also gave mankind complete authority over the earth itself. This authority was still in the hands of men after the Fall. During that window of time the psalmist said, "The heavens are the heavens of the LORD; But the earth He has given to the sons of men" (Ps. 115:16).

So let me explain the situation. Right after the Fall, God was in heaven, ruling heaven without any rebellion or contest present. Satan had taken mankind's authority and was using it to keep man from God. At the same time, mankind was still moving around on Earth in dominion, while separated from God.

As time went on, Satan used "his" authority to frustrate

man's attempt to interact with the Lord and eventually to confuse successive generations about the very nature of God. As Satan's deceptions ran deeper and deeper into the minds and hearts of men, eventually he convinced them that they should be worshiping things other than God. He then had his demons stand in for man's gods to receive their worship (1 Cor. 10:20). As they worshiped demons, men began to dedicate their lives, property, possessions, and children to them. By their devotion to demons, men gave the devil increasing authority and influence in the earth and in their own lives.

Satan used his ill-gotten, though legitimately held, authority to usurp mankind's earthly authority. He used the combination of authorities to do what he always does—steal, kill, and destroy (John 10:10). The devil's influence in the earth got so out of hand that "the wickedness of man was great on the earth, and *that every intent of the thoughts of his heart was only evil continually*" (Gen. 6:5, emphasis added).

As a child, I used to think that it was unfortunate that mankind no longer lived to be hundreds of years old, like they used to before the Flood (Gen. 6:3). Only after I began to understand the workings of the devil's influence in the earth did I realize that when God shortened man's lifespan it was an act of mercy rather than an act of judgment. Watch the full lifespan of the average unbeliever. Usually, they start out as innocent children, without any evil motive or intent. As they grow older, they incur wounds, make mistakes, and commit sins. This combination slowly corrupts the victim and transforms them into something more and more unlike the innocent children they started out as. We all know people who are now (if they are still living) in their eighties and nineties and are still in rebellion to God. These are often some of the most disturbingly bitter and angry individuals. Now, imagine a race of people who live with this corrupting influence for over nine hundred years. How miserable would that race be?

The Lord's response to such an awful situation was to wipe the earth clean and start over with Noah's family. It didn't take long for people to abandon the Lord in favor of subjugation to the devil all over again. The point I am trying to make is that Satan couldn't take all of man's earthly authority and therefore subjugate him all at once. It had to happen by degrees, because he needed mankind's consent. This holds true on an individual level as well. If Satan had his way, every child on Earth would be born completely possessed by demons.

The ugly part is that once a man gives some of his authority to a demon, he can't make the demon give it back. So, it really doesn't matter how unfair the demon is in his dealings with the man. Let me give an extreme example. Let's say a farmer owns a great deal of land and is having trouble getting it to produce adequate crops. So he goes to the local pagan temple and prays to the goddess there, asking her to come and bless his crops. He has, in effect, given a demonic spirit access to his land and crops. The spirit will likely come in and bless his crops for a year or two, but after a while it will use its access to blight his crops. The man will likely inquire of the goddess, asking why she isn't blessing his crops. She will then respond and say that he has been a less-than-adequate devotee of hers and will demand more worship, sacrifices, and attention. If he gives in to the spirit's demands, he will in effect be giving it even more access to his life, property, and family. Initially, the spirit will go back to being "nice" for a while, but it will eventually tighten the noose again to get ever more access. The man's only recourse was and still is to appeal to God.

Unfortunately, a person living before the time of Christ who tried to do anything spiritual was most likely to run into the world's primary high priest, Satan. From his place, Satan first tried to deceive people seeking a real spiritual experience into buying into an evil counterfeit. If that failed, then he very effectively accused them. (Remember, they were still under the bondage of sin.) When Christ came into the picture, He took His place as our High Priest and shared it with the church. Now in Christ, the accusations of the devil are worthless. Our cries, on the other hand, will always be heard by our loving Father, who just happens to be the almighty, omnipotent God, Creator of all things.

Because of Jesus, Satan no longer has the priestly authority that he gained from Adam. Currently, however, he still possesses some of his earthly authority. All of that authority has been gained from deceiving mankind, from deceiving people who knowingly or unknowingly agree to let him keep it. If, for instance, people actively agree with some of the lies of the enemy, then they end up granting the devil permission to act in accordance with those lies. When those people grow old and die, the devil will still remain in possession of that authority. The situation can and will continue on in that awful state for countless generations until the church steps up and changes things. This is where the real clashes of warfare begin.

On one side of the battle line stands the devil, his army of fallen angels, a great deal of authority in the earth (usurped from the hands of men), and a large number of deceived humans who are unknowingly doing the devil's bidding. On the other side stand the church, God almighty, and an innumerable host of angels. The church first goes before the Lord as priests and pleads that He will intervene in a situation with His mercy. Once the saints have the Lord's blessing, they take back the authority piece by piece. This may involve breaking all agreements between mankind and the demons in question, or it may involve asking God to forgive old sin issues that are still granting the spirits access. Once all of the demons' access to an area or person is removed, the church can command the devil to leave the situation, effectively giving up his influence. In this way, the church can take back everything that has ever fallen into the hands of our enemy.

Satan's lease has been up for two thousand years. It is a continual source of amazement to me that we, the superintendents of the world, the redeemed church, have just not bothered to evict him. It doesn't really matter if the people of the world continue to open their lives, property, families, and so forth up to the devil by not coming to the Lord. For many if not most of these people, we have the equipment necessary to prevent the devil from doing anything with or to them. Whether they may have opened the front door of their lives to a demon knowingly or unknowingly, that doesn't mean that we can't stop the demon dead in its tracks before it gets onto their front lawn.

The authority we have been given over the devil is extreme. Jesus said, "Behold, I have given you *authority* to tread on serpents and scorpions, and over *all* the power of the enemy, and nothing will injure you" (Luke 10:19, emphasis added). To put it another way, we have been given the authority to turn the god of this age into a doormat.

Chapter 8

AUTHORITY, PART 2

I N THE LAST CHAPTER WE TALKED ABOUT THE SOURCE
of authority and some of the ways that it can be hijacked
by the enemy of our souls. We also covered the impact of
Christ's sacrifice and how He has restored authority to us as
children of God.

In a spiritual sense, mankind is mostly used to walking
around in a state of powerlessness that is unnecessary, out of
accordance with the will of God, and just generally unbefit-
ting those of us with so high a calling. In this chapter, I have
sought to outline some general guidelines for using authority.
They amount to five basic principles that will give you a basic
understanding of how authority can and often does work on
a day-to-day basis. I can't give you specific solutions to every
single problem and situation that you will likely encounter;
no book is that big. If you want to know more about how to
apply these principles, your best option is to study the Word
of God and ask the Holy Spirit for understanding. As it says
in James 1:5, "If any man lacks wisdom let him ask of God."
My sincere hope is that after reading through and meditating
on this chapter you will have a framework for knowing how

authority can and should be used. From that framework, you will be better able to ask intelligent questions that will yield productive and useful answers.

Lesson 1: Pray

> "Pray, then, in this way: 'Our Father who is in heaven, Hallowed be Your name. 'Your kingdom come Your will be done, On earth as it is in heaven. Give us this day our daily bread. And forgive us our debts, as we also have forgiven our debtors. And do not lead us into temptation, but deliver us from evil. [For Yours is the kingdom and the power and the glory forever. Amen.]'"
>
> —MATTHEW 6:9–13

I love the Lord's Prayer so much that I feel like I could write a book on it. It was given to us as a model for how to pray. It also expresses a great deal of what we should pray for.

I would like to focus on the part of the prayer that says, "Your kingdom come Your will be done, On earth as it is in heaven." I believe that these are some of the most loaded words in all of Scripture. A kingdom is marked by one thing, the presence of a king. In His kingdom, His desires and commands will be fulfilled on Earth just like they are in heaven.

So often we encounter problems on Earth and we ask ourselves if it is God's will to intervene. We know that if we pray according to His will He will act accordingly, so we want to be sure that we are in agreement with Him before we take a stand in faith. Too often we psych ourselves out of answered prayer because we think the Lord's will is a mystery. So often we think the troubles we face might be His will when all too frequently the exact opposite is true. Most of the world's problems are rooted in a rebellion against God on the part of its inhabitants, be they human or demon. The rebellion and its consequences are the things that are outside of God's will.

Remember, heaven is a place that always bends to the will of God. If you ever want a general rule of thumb to know His will, then just ask yourself, What's heaven like? Is there sickness in heaven? What about poverty and lack? Is there confusion or despair? Tell me, is there any injustice in heaven? Is there unforgiveness in heaven? Does the devil routinely have his way there? The answer is a resounding no! To put it bluntly, heaven is a paradise beyond our wildest imaginings; it is also the only place that functions exactly as God desires at every second of every day. So anything on Earth that does not currently live up to the reality of heaven is a valid reason to pray and expect divine intervention.

I will, however, provide one caveat. His solutions to the problems that we face can be a bit different from the ones that we expect. Jesus performed the same miracles a number of different ways. He commanded some people to be healed. He laid hands on others. He even spit on at least one person. In general, when you come across situations needing the power of God, assume it is His will to do something to fix the situation. Then begin to ask Him how He wants to go about it. By walking with the Lord in this way, you will begin to learn how He has designed you to function and how He likes to function through you. That whole ministry will become part of your relationship with the Lord. It will become a natural flow.

Warfare against the demonic is part of my walk with the Lord. I have come to know our God as the Lord of hosts, and I have also come to know my place in His army. Right now I am very much learning my place as a writer and a teacher, and I am seeing Him as the Author and Finisher of our faith as well as the Teacher who leads and guides us into all truth.

In the title, I promised a discussion about how to use authority. I started off with prayer for a good reason. Believe it or not, when we pray even the most timid of prayers, we are using our authority. A prayer is a legally binding invitation to the Lord to have access to something, with the expectation that He will use His all-surpassing power to accomplish some purpose. Though you may not realize it, by simply talking to the Lord once in a while you wield an immense amount of authority in the earth and have some influence over how the Creator of all will use His immeasurable power.

So, to sum up the first lesson in using authority: pray according to the will of God. If you find you do need more information concerning His specific will on a matter, then "ask that you may be filled with the knowledge of His will in all spiritual wisdom and understanding," (Col. 1:9). Develop your relationship with Him in the areas in which you are regularly encountering obstacles.

Lesson 2: Command

From time to time I find that I end up in situations where simply asking the Lord to do something won't get the job done. That is when it is time to issue commands (or decrees, if you prefer). The Lord gave us authority with the intent that we would use it to accomplish His purposes in the earth.

He calls us "*kings* and priests" (Rev. 1:6, KJV, emphasis added). Like all kings, we have been given a place where *we* have dominion. Psalm 115:16 declares, "The earth He has given to the sons of men." There are times when it is appropriate to literally command something to happen.

Our authority is derived from our Creator, who put us in charge down here on Earth, and from our Savior, whose sacrifice continues to guarantee our relationship with Himself. So when issuing a command, it is usually appropriate—and advisable—to declare it in the name of Jesus. You might wish to follow the following model: "In the name of Jesus, I command (insert the thing you are commanding to happen)."

Anything under your authority has to obey your commands. Occasionally, you may run into something that should obey you but decides not to. I, for instance, occasionally run in to demons that aren't quick to leave when I tell them to. That is when I call on the resources of heaven that are available to me to enforce my own orders. A good starting point, should you run into this kind of situation, is simply to ask the Lord to back you up. In this sort of case, I usually specify the type of backup I want, which is to have warring angels come and drive/escort the demonic forces out of my presence. Occasionally, the requested backup just doesn't do the job. When this happens, it is usually because someone (possibly me) has given them some root of access. Usually the Lord will tell you what needs to be done to revoke that access.

The influence of your authority goes beyond demons. I recently found that I had a fairly large amount of repressed anger in my heart that was coming out in all sorts of quiet yet unpleasant ways. I tried commanding the anger to leave. I also asked the Lord to heal the root of it. I got nowhere. Then I started asking the Lord what was going on. He pointed out that I was walking in unforgiveness toward a small number of people. When we walk in unforgiveness we walk outside of the covenant. To whatever degree we are outside of the covenant, we lose all access to power and authority. It is very much like Samson right after Delilah cut his hair. He went out as before, thinking he was going to destroy his enemies. He lost all too quickly. Living outside the covenant can be very costly. Like Samson, I did some repenting, which in my case included some forgiving of others. As my authority under the covenant became functional again, my previous edict to remove anger became enforceable and the anger left.

Just like in prayer, we need to walk with the Lord when we issue commands. This is all part of building our relationship with Him. We need to get to know Him as the God and King whose Word is law, and we need to see ourselves as His chosen ambassadors who have been sent to represent Him in the earth. As we walk with the Lord, He gives us greater and greater access to the resources of heaven.

Lesson 3: Live

Live your life, make decisions, and have opinions. You are royalty. (Remember, you are a royal priesthood.) You may not feel like royalty most days. You may not think that you are royalty, but the fact remains whether you like it or not. Your very opinions, thoughts, feelings, and your day-to-day decisions carry great influence.

Every angel is fully aware of the tremendous position you have in Christ. They are called to be ministering spirits to those who would be heirs of salvation; that's us (Heb. 1:14). They are literally our servants. An angel who has been assigned to me will aid me in any way he can, in anything I endeavor to do, so long as it is in the will of God. When I make a decision and start walking according to it, because I am a child of the King, all that is around me in the spiritual realm is affected.

Knowing this, we need to choose to make decisions. We need to seek the Lord's opinion and will concerning all things.

> In all thy ways acknowledge him, and he shall direct thy paths.
>
> —PROVERBS 3:5–6, KJV

We need to also be mindful that He wants us to make some of our own decisions as well, for there are times He will give us a choice rather than an order. For example, during a time of mass hysteria and distrust toward God, Caleb was faithful, so he was given the choice of where he wanted to dwell in the Promised Land. The Lord let him choose his own inheritance (Josh. 14). The Scriptures say that God appoints the times, places, and seasons of our lives (Eccles. 3:1); yet,

He let Caleb choose his own place and property, as well as the place and property of his kids for generations to come.

In short, we need to live with the Lord, knowing that He is on our side. We obey anything He tells us to do because we know we can trust His commands. We can confidently make decisions when He doesn't give clear orders or when His orders say to make a choice of our own because we can trust Him to take care of us at all times.

Lesson 4: Do not give anything to the devil

Don't give the devil or any of his demons any form of access to any part of your life, property, possessions, relationships, destiny, finances, or children. Paul put it this way, "Do not give the devil an opportunity" (Eph. 4:27). Every decision we make and even the ones we leave unmade affect what God's angels and Satan's demons can do. With that in mind, we need to make every effort to make spiritually wise decisions.

If you use your authority foolishly and give the devil access to your life, he will use his new open door to find opportunity to put you in bondage.

Lesson 5: Recovering something given to the devil

If you find that the devil has acquired access to something, revoke it. This is especially useful if you find you have been negligent in carrying out lesson four, but it can also apply in other circumstances as well. This is usually not complicated or difficult, but it does pay to know how he got his authority in each situation. What follows is a quick list of ways that you can end up giving access to your life to the demonic horde and a simple tactic for revoking their access. In the next chapter I will cover some of the ways that people open up access for the devil to affect each other's lives.

Unforgiveness

Our whole covenant with God is based on forgiveness. He demands that we forgive others. If we disobey Him in this and choose not to forgive, then He will not forgive us (Matt. 6:14). This is the covenant. If we choose to walk and live in unforgiveness, then we render our own covenant with God ineffective. If we are walking in rejection of God's covenant, then we are automatically embracing something else.

If the Lord reveals to you that you are walking in unforgiveness, you need to immediately do three things before you even address your enemy.

- You need to acknowledge your sin and apologize to the Lord.

- You need to extend forgiveness to the person in question.

- You need to ask the Lord if you need to do something in the natural to go along with this. If you have been walking in unforgiveness toward someone, you will likely have treated them poorly in some fashion. You may need to tell them you forgive them and ask for their forgiveness in return.

Regarding the last step: it may not always be possible to carry out all the Lord asks in the moment He asks it or all that you agree to the moment you agree to it. Hannah made an agreement that she would give her firstborn son back to the Lord once He gave one to her. The Lord allowed her to conceive a child, but she couldn't very well leave him (Samuel) in the tabernacle with Eli right away; he had to be born and then weaned first (1 Sam. 1–2). If you make an agreement with the Lord to fix what needs fixing, the acknowledgment of what is wrong and the promise to do what is appropriate to fix it at the first opportunity is usually all that is needed to be able to drive out the enemy in the short run. In the long run you will need to follow through on your plans if you want to sustain your freedom.

Habitual sin

When we first start to sin, often the Holy Spirit will come along to convict us. If we stay in our sin and do not respond appropriately to His conviction, He may leave us alone in that area of our lives. At this point it really doesn't matter what the sin is; it can be wrong attitudes like jealousy or self-pity, or it can involve actions that you know the Lord doesn't approve of. If we deliberately allow sin to have place in our lives, then by default we also agree to endure the consequences of our sin. These consequences will often involve some form of demonic access to our lives.

The simple solution is to get right with God. Repent and vow to live totally for the Lord, especially in the area in question. Then you can address the enemy and have them removed. Frequently, the enemy will try to hang around for a while to see if you are serious. This is where you need to follow James's instruction, "Submit yourselves therefore to God. Resist the devil, and he will flee from you" (James 4:7). If you fall back into your sin, be quick to repent. As long as you are resisting the sin and endeavoring to submit to God—in other words, you haven't given up—you are in a place from which you can fight, and thus, you can drive every demon out.

Dabbling in the occult or other false religions

Any instance of willingly interacting with a spiritual power other than God can fall under this category. There are definitely degrees of severity here. On the light side I would put playing with Ouija boards, reading horoscopes, and getting a psychic reading. These are usually instances in which the participant is willingly yet passively engaged with the enemy. If you go to get a psychic reading you are opening yourself up to the demonic to read your life like a book. The psychic is the one who is actively engaged in dealing with the demon or demons in question. On the fairly serious side I would put membership in a cult, astral projection, low-level Wicca, or membership in any religion other than Christianity (or Judaism). These are deeds where the participant has to actively and personally engage the demonic. This means that they actually open up some sort of communion or fellowship with an evil spirit. At this level, the person in question does not usually know that they are actually dealing with demons. They may think that they are using their own innate abilities, that they are talking to "friendly" spirits or gods of some sort, or that they are interacting with the universal, cosmic what have you. At the really ugly end of the spectrum is open, high-level witchcraft, voodoo, shamanism, etc. At these levels, the participants know that they are dealing with spirits that can be and often are dangerous. Many of them are aware that they are dealing with demons. Many people at this level realize that the God we serve is in direct opposition to their gods/spirits.

In all cases, the former participant should repent of their deeds and ask the Lord to cleanse them. They will also want to break the fellowship and any unspoken agreements that they had with the demonic. They should also formally renounce any clearly stated agreements that they may have had with various spirits. They should destroy or at least get rid of every object related to their occult activities. They should also command the complete destruction of anything that may have been implanted into their lives by the demonic. After that, it is time to start addressing the enemy and telling him it is time to leave. I recommend having a few trustworthy friends who are familiar with this sort of thing around while going through this deliverance. If you have been pretty deep in the occult, you will almost certainly want their help and support.

Sexual sin

There are only two ways to change your basic identity. One is to accept Christ.

> If anyone is in Christ, he is a new creation.
> —2 CORINTHIANS 5:17, NIV

The next is through sexual union.

Therefore shall a man leave his father and his mother, and shall cleave unto his wife: and they shall be one flesh.

—Genesis 2:24, kjv

Through intercourse, the participants go from being separate to being joined both physically (for the moment) and spiritually for life. If this union is carried out on the enemy's terms, the consequences are usually tragic. In general, where the demonic has had rights to oppress one of the individuals, their union creates a wide bridge of access that the demons in question can freely cross over to oppress the other individual.

The participant needs first to repent to the Lord for anything that was biblically wrong with the relationship. Generally, this falls under one of two categories: either the union happened between two people who were not married to each other or the marriage was not founded on Christ. The participant should also address what was wrong with his or her thinking and approach that got them into the relationship in the first place. Then the individual needs to command himself or herself spiritually severed from the person he or she was wrongly in union with. After this, I recommend asking the Lord to cleanse them both of any remaining parts of each other and then ask the Lord to reassemble each of them as whole individuals, as they were before they got together. Then the former participant should be able to adequately drive off any leftover demonic influence from the relationship itself.

They may still need to deal with leftover emotional pain from a relationship gone awry, but more about that later.

Agreeing with the enemy

I am not talking about making formal agreements with demons. That falls under the occult section. The agreement here is about what you believe. If you decide to believe something in your heart, then you actually empower it to come into being. You will also live in accordance with your beliefs, and your actions will lend further weight to the matter. When that belief is in agreement with God, we usually call it faith. The presence or absence of this spiritually quantifiable belief actually allows or restrains the manifestation of the miraculous power of Jesus (Mark 6:4–6). If your beliefs will allow or restrain the Lord of glory, you can bet that they are potent enough to allow or restrain the manifestation of the demonic.

If you are in agreement with something not of the Lord, then you can bet that there is a demon around somewhere who is willing and eager to act on your beliefs. This usually leads to patterns of failure and trouble in life or to specific bad outcomes, not to a deep-seated oppression. On a one-on-one basis, our enemy will expend a great deal of energy trying to convince us of various lies because they directly equate to specific points of access into our lives.

On a day-to-day basis we need to meditate on the Word and allow a daily renewal of our minds (Josh. 1:8; Rom. 12:2). This will tend to root these wrong beliefs out, as well as prevent them from forming in the first place.

When we come across wrong beliefs, we need to be quick

to change them. If you have reason to suspect that the enemy has been actively exploiting an old belief, then that belief should be verbally renounced and the new belief should be stated out loud. The new belief should be directly verifiable in Scripture. If the new belief isn't based on Scripture, then all you are doing is trading one bondage for another. After the beliefs are straightened out, then just address the enemy and tell them to quit doing whatever it was they were doing and to go away.

Unresolved trauma or emotional pain

As part of life on this earth, we all encounter events that bring emotional pain. These can include losing a loved one, enduring physical and emotional abuse, betrayal, and abandonment. Usually these pains catch us off guard, and they force us to reevaluate what we think we know about ourselves, the world around us, our relationships, and our God. If we are not extremely careful, we can and often do this reevaluating out of the place of our pain and not out of the Word of God. Guess which one leads to life and which one leads to bondage.

In order to heal from past hurts, we need to get the truth of the matter from God, and we need to allow Him to come into that hurting place in our hearts and heal it.

On occasion, spirits of trauma will come in to remind the person of his or her pain and to pick at the wound. Once the hurt is dealt with, this kind usually leaves on its own. If you happen to find an exception to this trend, you can always forcibly kick it out, though I recommend asking God if you are overlooking some important detail first.

In all of these cases, there is great potential for overlap. It is possible that getting freedom in any area may require dealing with the enemy on several different levels. In the case of trauma, usually unforgiveness and wrong beliefs come into play.

While we are talking about forgiveness, don't forget to forgive yourself and to forgive the Lord if you have been angry with Him.

Chapter 9

HOW THE HORDES FUNCTION

ONE FACT ABOUT OUR ENEMY HAS NEVER CEASED to amaze me. They are an almost numberless mob of the most hateful, spiteful, deceived, and selfish individuals in creation; yet, they somehow manage to function in some form of unity in strength and purpose. They actually manage to maintain an organizational hierarchy. The Lord was very gracious to us when He gave Paul the understanding of how they functioned.

> For our struggle is not against flesh and blood, but against the rulers, against the powers, against the world forces of this darkness, against the spiritual forces of wickedness in the heavenly places.
> —EPHESIANS 6:12

There is only one challenge with this verse. It is almost impossible to directly translate it in a way that gives the reader a clear understanding as to how each position in the hierarchy actually functions. To make matters worse, many translations choose some of the same words and apply them to different positions. When several translations are viewed side by side, they appear to be nothing more than random lists of governmental positions, possibly in different orders. To clear up the confusion, we are going to break them down in the Greek, one position at a time.

Arché

Most versions of the Bible translate the first position, the *arché* (pronounced "ar-khay"), as either "rulers" or "principalities." Many commentators, as well as most people I've heard speak on the subject, end up using "principalities." The third position, "world forces of this darkness," is more frequently rendered "rulers over the darkness of this earth." So we have two positions called rulers. In order to minimize confusion, I am going to keep the transliteration *arché* throughout the rest of this book, and I will use my own names for the other positions where I believe it will be helpful.

Arché means "ruler" or "beginning." An *arché* is a personified source of authority in the demonic realms. In our modern forms of governance, they are akin to a legislative branch; they make the rules and policies that everyone else lives by. When one of these guys is in power, they tell all of the demons under them how things are to function and what they as a group are going to try to accomplish.

In general, an *arché* is a spirit that has somehow acquired control of a point of access through which they can affect more than one human. These spirits are powerful enough to command a number of other, lesser demons. When they operate in the life of only one person, we call them strongmen (Matt. 12:29).

In order to bring about deliverance to a person, place, or group of people, the *arché* will always have to be confronted.

Powers

In virtually all circumstances, the word *exousia* (pronounced "ex-oo-see`-ah") is translated as "power." The word can actually mean "strength," "might," or "power." In a governmental sense it refers to the authority and power that has been delegated to this person from a higher place in the hierarchy.

In our modern government systems, this is the executive branch and function of the government. This person does not make the laws but is responsible for carrying them out. In terms of a monarchy, a power would be some sort of emissary to the king, possibly an ambassador or a general.

In the demonic system, power comes from possessing the points of access to the human realms. Whichever spirit possesses the access is automatically deemed the *arché*. The *arché* will delegate specific authority, rights, and responsibilities to their powers. If you are dealing with a direct frontal assault from the demonic, it is usually a power that is doing the work.

Just like any other spirit, a power can be stopped dead in its tracks. Beyond a very short term gain, it does not usually do a lot of good to pay too much attention to the powers. As soon as you repel one power, the *arché* can just send another. For the patient, it is possible to repel every last one of an *arché*'s powers, but even that does not fix the problem; the *arché* will just appoint more. If you want to decisively win the battle at hand, your best option is to go after the source of the problem, which is the *arché*.

We will get into the details of removing an *arché* in the next chapter.

Kosmokratore

Sometimes translated as the "world forces of this darkness" or the "rulers over the darkness of this earth," *kosmokratore* (pronounced "kos-mok-rat'-ore") is from two separate roots. *Kosmos* means "world" and can also refer to the order upon which it is built and functions. We get our modern word *cosmos* from the ancient Greek word *kosmos*. *Kratistos* literally means "strongest." So literally, *kosmokratore* means "strongest in all the world." These are the large, unpleasant, world-ruling spirits.

Satan himself certainly falls under this category. Deities of religions that are still widely practiced today, like Allah from Islam and Brahma (along with Vishnu and Shiva) from Hinduism, are also clearly world rulers. Major ungodly movements often have their roots in these sorts of spirits. Communism was more than a repressive form of governance; it was an atheistic movement that set itself directly in opposition to God during the twentieth century. Clearly its source was of an evil origin. In the same century, fascism brought on World War II.

There are a couple of quieter world rulers that work more behind the scenes. A powerful demonic spirit called the queen of heaven is currently in control of much of the world's wealth. The major spirit of anti-Semitism is also a world ruler; for two thousand years it has managed to stir up fierce opposition to the Jews all over the world.

In his second canonized letter to the Corinthians, Paul writes, "Our gospel is…veiled to those who are perishing, in whose case the god of this world has blinded the minds of the unbelieving so that they might not see the light of the gospel of the glory of Christ, who is the image of God" (2 Cor. 4:3–4). The successful fulfillment of the Great Commission, making disciples of all nations, requires that people actually see the value of the gospel so as to be willing to be discipled by its communicators. For the blinded, lost minds of the world to see, the god of this age (Satan) and his world-ruling representatives will have to be dethroned.

If we would follow the Lord's primary instruction for evangelism, we will have considerably more success in our efforts. His model was quite simple: "The harvest is plentiful, but the laborers are few; therefore beseech the Lord of the harvest to send out laborers into His harvest" (Luke 10:2). Did you catch it? The first thing we do is beseech the Lord. Most translations use the word *pray*. We need to pray first, then go into the harvest as the Lord sends us. As we pray, the blinding influence of this world's dark rulers is neutralized and minds and hearts are prepared by the Holy Spirit for the message of the gospel.

Spirits that have sway over a great part of the earth are not spirits that should be engaged personally by individual believers or even in small groups. If we submit ourselves to the Lord and walk in obedience to Him, we are promised a tremendous blessing in our battles and struggles.

> But you will chase your enemies and they will fall
> before you by the sword; five of you will chase a
> hundred, and a hundred of you will chase ten thou-
> sand, and your enemies will fall before you by the
> sword.
>
> —LEVITICUS 26:7–8

The verse does not say that an individual will take it upon himself to go solo against a host of 6 billion plus demons and win without effort. The only way we are effectively going to remove them is if we work together on a large, corporate scale. The encouraging news is that there is a groundswell of a prayer movement that is moving through the world right now, and this movement has the potential to dethrone every last world ruler. Our job as individuals is to join with our brothers and sisters and pray, pray, pray until the Lord's will is done in the earth like it is in heaven.

GENERAL SPIRITUAL WICKEDNESS IN HEAVENLY PLACES

I like to call these spirits *wickednesses*. These are your typical evil spirits. Sometimes they roam about on their own just looking for opportunities to harass people. More often, they are serving the purposes of other, more powerful spirits. In my experience, they frequently attach themselves to various powers. These are also the spirits that seek their own personal access into the lives of individuals. These are the kind of spirits that get cast out of people. They can exist alone or in groups. Jesus encountered a possessed person who had so many demons that they decided it was more expedient to call themselves Legion rather than answer individually (Matt. 5:9).

These are not usually very powerful spirits. They can, however, become pesky to remove if they find a unique point of access that is difficult for the believers in question to identify. That's when they take on the qualities of an *arché* or strongman. Depending on the nature of the strongman and its particular point of access, they can have several spirits under them. The most effective way to deal with them is to address the point of access. That's when it becomes imperative to walk closely with the Lord. He knows all things and can show you what to do to take back that point of access and thus be free from the demonic.

Ninety-nine percent of the warfare that we encounter is with these wickednesses. Their main method of attack is to plant thoughts in the minds of people or to flood them with an emotional feeling, usually along the lines of fear, stress, or anger. The first thing that must be learned to adequately deal with them is to understand that not every thought that enters your mind is from you.

Sometimes the thoughts that enter our minds are from the Lord. Jesus was walking along with His disciples. He turned and asked them, "Who do people say that I am?" (Matt. 16:13, author's paraphrase). The disciples started answering out of what they had heard people say: Elijah, John the Baptist raised from the dead, a prophet, etc. Then He asked them, "Who do you say that I am?"

> Simon Peter answered, "You are the Christ, the Son of the living God." And Jesus said to him, "Blessed

> are you, Simon Barjona, because flesh and blood did not reveal this to you, but My Father who is in heaven."
>
> —MATTHEW 16:15–17

Peter thought he had figured out on his own that Jesus was the Messiah, but Jesus was quick to tell him that some of what he knew, and therefore some of what he thought, was directly from the Holy Spirit.

Sadly, demons can plant thoughts in much the same way. A few verses later, Jesus started to explain to His disciples that He would be killed and raised from the dead. Peter got all in a huff and took Him aside to rebuke Him.

> "God forbid it, Lord! This shall never happen to You." But He turned and said to Peter, "Get behind Me, Satan! You are a stumbling block to Me; for you are not setting your mind on God's interests, but man's."
>
> —MATTHEW 16:22–23

So what do we do? We have our thoughts, God's thoughts, and demonic thoughts that can enter our minds at any moment. The first thing we need to do is to cultivate a vital relationship with the Godhead. We need to know Him as our Shepherd, the one who leads us, protects us, and feeds us. "The sheep know the Shepherd's voice," the Scriptures tell us (John 10:4, author's paraphrase). We can think thoughts that are worthless or even harmful. Demons will certainly throw as much of the harmful thoughts our way as possible. To make progress in this area, I don't

recommend spending a lot of time trying to tell the difference between your thoughts and your enemies'. Rather, I
recommend getting to know your Shepherd's thoughts and
spending time coming into agreement with Him. As we get
to know His thoughts, we can join with Paul in saying, "For
though we walk in the flesh, we do not war according to the
flesh, for the weapons of our warfare are not of the flesh,
but divinely powerful for the destruction of fortresses. We
are destroying speculations and every lofty thing raised
up against the knowledge of God, and we are taking every
thought captive to the obedience of Christ" (2 Cor. 10:3–5).
The point is to bring every thought (regardless of its source)
into obedience to Christ.

Over time as our thoughts come into agreement with
those of Jesus, then those thoughts that come from demonic
sources will stick out like sore thumbs. Sometimes particular demonic thoughts are one-time events, like what Peter
experienced. When they come, just reject them from your
conscious mind and move on. For more persistent demonic
thoughts, the first step is to make sure that you are in
disagreement with the thought (take it captive). Then you
may need to address the demonic spirit and order it to leave
in the name of Jesus.

The daily Christian walk should bring us into closer and
closer agreement with the Lord. Imagine living a life in
which every thought you think is in agreement with what is
pleasing to the Lord. Consider this:

> Without faith it is impossible to please Him, for he who comes to God must believe that He is and that He is a rewarder of those who seek Him.
> —Hebrews 11:6

Imagine if every thought you think were a thought of faith. It would mean a life of unimaginable power, because faith like a mustard seed can move mountains. It would also be a life of unparalleled closeness to God. How awesome would that be? I don't know about you, but I am aiming my life in that direction. By the end of my life, I may not have reached the point where every thought is in agreement with Him, but I intend to be a whole lot closer then than I am now.

Chapter 10

HOW THE HORDES DO NOT FUNCTION

I FIND ONE THING ABOVE ALL OTHERS TO BE A REAL frustration in wrestling with our mostly invisible enemies: they are mostly invisible. Our task of dethroning them would sure be a lot easier if we could see them. For that matter, just dealing with attacks would be a piece of cake if we knew where they were coming from before they arrived.

Fortunately, the Lord has put three aids in place to help us deal with the problem of invisibility. One, He occasionally opens our eyes to see what is going on in the spiritual realms (2 Kings 6:17). Two, He will tell us what we need to know (John 15:15). Three, He has provided us with a number of situations that are analogous to spiritual warfare. The first two helpful things are entirely dependent upon your relationship with the Lord. There isn't much I can tell you other than to keep walking with Him. There are no shortcuts on that road. Regarding the third aid, I can give you some useful observations from the Scriptures.

We call it warfare for a reason. When we talk about spiritual warfare we usually quote passages out of Ephesians 6

("We wrestle not against flesh and blood...," v. 12, KJV). Paul didn't come up with this imagery all by himself. I don't even think he thought it was some great big revelation. I imagine Paul thought of it as a natural extension of the Scriptures that he had grown up reading. God placed war-related imagery all over the pages of the Bible. There are well over fifty instances of the words *arrow* or *arrows*—an implement of war—alone. All of them are in the Old Testament, and many of them are obviously figurative or spiritual in nature. If looking at the quantity of battles and war imagery doesn't get your attention, maybe this will: the Lord calls himself the Lord of hosts (you could translate *hosts* as "armies") more often than any other specific title.

I contend that one of the best ways to get a picture of the demonic army in action is to look at the armies and battles of the Old Testament. If you want to know some good strategies, find out what the Lord had Israel employ against their enemies.

Did you know that the Lord feels no compulsion to fight "fair" with His enemies? Let's look at His strategy for taking the Promised Land. First, he gave the land's inhabitants an overwhelming sense of dread.

> "This day I will begin to put the dread and fear of
> you upon the peoples everywhere under the heavens,
> who, when they hear the report of you, will tremble
> and be in anguish because of you."
> —DEUTERONOMY 2:25

Prolonged stress (like we see here in the form of fear) wreaks havoc on the body. This is psychological warfare. Then when the day of battle arrives He throws them into confusion (Deut. 7:23). So the Lord's weapons in this situation were fear, stress, physical fatigue (resulting from prolonged stress and fear), psychological fatigue (also as a result of prolonged stress and fear), and then confusion at critical moments.

There are times where the Lord asks His people to cooperate with Him in the fear and confusion process. During the time of the judges the Lord picked a man named Gideon to kill off the Midianite army. He told Gideon to arm his army of three hundred men with swords, clay pots, torches, and horns. They snuck up on the Midianites at nighttime. The Lord allowed Gideon to overhear a conversation between two Midianites; in their conversation one relayed a dream to the other. The one who heard the dream interpreted it to mean that Gideon's army would kill them all. God had already put His dread on them.

Gideon's army took up positions all around the Midianite camp with their lit torches concealed beneath their clay pots. At a set signal all the pots were broken, suddenly revealing a great deal of light. Then all Gideon's men sounded their trumpets and shouted at the top of their lungs. Armies usually used horns and other loud instruments to communicate with their troops. A general would only take along multiple trumpets if he had a particularly large army (who might not hear just one trumpet). Gideon took three hundred trumpets, giving the impression that he had an unimaginably large army with him, when nothing could be further from the truth. Then the Lord topped it off by throwing the

Midianites into confusion and panic to such an extent that they started killing each other.

The Lord will also trick His enemies through their over-confidence. As Israel was taking the Promised Land, they came to a city called Ai. They attacked it and lost. It turned out that Israel had sinned, and therefore the Lord was not going to support them. After they took care of the sin issue, the Lord gave them a plan for taking the city. A group of warriors was placed behind the city, while the majority of the army attacked from the front. The attacking army pretended to be beaten and ran from the battle. The residents of Ai, figuring that they had won again, pulled together every man in the city to pursue the Israelites. After they left the city unguarded, the hidden group of warriors ran into the city, ransacked it, and set it on fire. Then they ran after the men of Ai, who found themselves completely surrounded by the Israelite army.

Gideon and Joshua both won major battles by God-autho-rized trickery and deception. Yet the best ruse of all time was pulled off by Jesus against Satan. Remember, He goaded Satan into killing Him. The Scriptures are plain:

> We speak God's wisdom in a mystery…which none of the rulers of this age has understood; for if they had understood it they would not have crucified the Lord of glory.
>
> —1 CORINTHIANS 2:7–8

Our God will take advantage of our enemies' weaknesses and mistakes in His battle plans. More than once, He has had them reveal to me their points of access. At that point, the battle is over as far as I'm concerned. It is just a process of cleanup from there on out.

On one occasion, the Lord gave a group of us revelation about a specific place we had been warring for in prayer. Apparently, the reigning *arché* was not well loved by his followers. (We didn't like him either.) In fact, one of those followers was in the process of leading an insurrection against him. If we would have let the insurrection take its course, either the *arché* or the leader of the insurrection would have been kicked out of the territory, along with a few of his closest supporters. However, the Lord had a better idea. The *arché*, by definition, was the demonic source for all of the demons' legal rights to exist and operate in that territory. For a demon to be there legally, they had to submit to the *arché*. Because of the insurrection, half the demonic army was no longer submitted to the *arché* and therefore no longer had legal rights to reside in that region. Since they didn't have any right to be there, all we had to do was order them to leave. As a result, the rebelling half of the demonic population in that region was removed in the matter of a few minutes.

As wonderful as it is when the Lord does something unexpected and bad for our enemies, the biblical model doesn't require us to take up a passive stance and wait for Him to get the ball rolling. David was a wonderful leader and is known for being a man after God's heart, yet he had an awfully turbulent reign. At one point, Absalom, one of his own sons, conspired to steal the kingdom. He nearly succeeded, partly because one of David's best advisors, Ahithophel, joined the conspiracy.

> Now someone told David, saying, "Ahithophel is among the conspirators with Absalom." And David said, "O LORD, I pray, make the counsel of Ahithophel foolishness."
>
> —2 SAMUEL 15:31

Right after that, David sent Hushai, one of his old advisors, to "join" the conspiracy in order to thwart the counsel of Ahithophel and to spy on Absalom.

In answer to David's prayer, Hushai was accepted as an advisor into Absalom's court and was given the opportunity to publicly disagree with Ahithophel's advice.

> Then Absalom and all the men of Israel said, "The counsel of Hushai...is better than the counsel of Ahithophel." For the LORD had ordained to thwart the good counsel of Ahithophel, so that the LORD might bring calamity on Absalom.
>
> —2 SAMUEL 17:14

David didn't wait. He made the first move in requesting that God bring down the advice of Ahithophel. Then when the opportunity presented itself, he sent Hushai to act in agreement with his prayer. We see that God gladly acted in accordance with David's requests to debilitate his enemies.

Elisha the prophet found himself in a situation to make a similar request. He had spent the last few years telling the king of Israel everything his enemy the king of Aram was about to do. The king of Aram eventually figured out that Elisha's prophetic gift was the reason that he continually lost all his battles. So, the king of Aram sent his army to capture Elisha. Just as they were about to get to Elisha's house he said, "'Strike this people with blindness I pray.' So He struck them with blindness according to the word of Elisha" (2 Kings 6:18).

In the last chapter, I said that it amazes me that a countless army of the most dysfunctional beings in existence can somehow function together as a unit. There is, however, one little fact that they would rather you didn't know: their unity is very fragile. Their dysfunction gets the better of them more often than they would like to admit. Most demons don't even think about the war as a whole; they just see their little piece of territory, and they spend a lot of time trying to expand their power and influence within it. They are consumed by their own selfishness, hatred, jealousy, strife, etc. Look at it this way. The fruit of the Spirit's work in our lives is "love, joy, peace, patience, kindness, goodness, faithfulness, gentleness, self-control" (Gal. 5:22). They rejected the Holy Spirit's influence thousands of years ago. They have no love, no joy, no peace, no patience, no kindness, no goodness, no faithfulness, no gentleness, and no self-control.

To further expound on what just the absence of love means, they have the exact opposite of everything love is in 1 Corinthians 13. So, a loveless demon is impatient, unkind, and is jealous. It brags, is arrogant, and acts unbecomingly. It seeks its own, is easily provoked, takes into account every wrong suffered, rejoices in unrighteousness, and despises the truth. It bears nothing, believes nothing, hopes nothing, and willingly endures nothing.

An organization made of people like that isn't going to be very organized or unified. The only thing that keeps demons from continuously warring against each other is a common enemy—us. I have used this fact to my advantage on numerous occasions. If I know I am about to deal with something particularly serious, I ask the Lord to break down their unity and to send fear and confusion. I also ask Him to help them make mistakes that I can take advantage of.

If you read the passages where the Lord puts His dread on His enemies, you find that the dread is usually based entirely on the reputation that the Lord has built through the testimonies of victories in this person's life. Rahab gave an insider's perspective on what the people of Jericho were thinking a few days before the Israelites took the city.

> I know that the LORD has given you the land, and that the terror of you has fallen on us, and that all the inhabitants of the land have melted away before you. For we have heard how the LORD dried up the water of the Red Sea before you when you came out of Egypt, and what you did to the two kings of the Amorites who were beyond the Jordan, to Sihon and Og, whom you utterly destroyed. When we heard it, our hearts melted and no courage remained in any man any longer because of you; for the LORD your God, He is God in heaven above and on earth beneath.
>
> —JOSHUA 2:9–11

More than once, I have found it advantageous to recite the victories of God to new demonic challengers. I believe that this is an essential skill that the church must learn, because we are called to overcome by the blood of the Lamb *and* the Word of our testimony (Rev. 12:11).

My only advice here is to keep the focus on Christ and what He did, not on your part in it. It is not a good idea to expound on our own greatness to a demon, because then we are walking in pride, which plays into their hands. Yet, if we walk in true humility, giving all the glory to God, we fight from a secure place.

Chapter 11

ARCHÉ REMOVAL

IF YOU WANT TO KILL A WEED, YOU HAVE TO DESTROY IT at the root. If you cut off the leaves, they will grow again. Plucking out the stem usually won't do it, either. You can run over most weeds with a lawn mower, and they will come right back along with your grass.

If you want to dismantle the larger networks of the demonic, the same principle applies. You have to take out the network at its source, the *arché*. Because of their importance, I have devoted this entire chapter to explaining how to permanently remove them.

As we covered in the last two chapters, the *arché* is the spirit that actually possesses the legal point of entry into the world. Every other demon in the network derives its authority directly from the *arché*. Usually the *arché* is the most intelligent and most powerful demon in the network as well, which is why many in the church are afraid to take them on. I believe that while a healthy respect for the activities of spiritual warfare is advisable, the outright refusal to take on even the most powerful *arché* is unfounded and unscriptural.

Archés always get their authority from humans. In some cases, that authority (or access, if you prefer) was given thousands of years ago, and sometimes it is actively being reapplied every day by the current population in an area. If an entire human population under the influence of an *arché* decided to gather together and turn from the *arché* to the Lord, you would see a much larger version of what we talked about in the last chapter. It would be a very easy deliverance, indeed.

Usually, whole populations are not ready to do this at any point in time. Therefore, the church is called on to act as priests in the earth. Remember, a priest represents God to man and man to God. Anyone who witnesses to the lost or ministers to a brother is walking in this ministry. We can, as priests, step in for a group of people and ask whatever we want from the Lord for their sake.

While the Israelites were wandering around in the desert, they had an episode of particularly unreasonable murmuring against Moses and Aaron. The Lord responded by releasing a plague with the intent of destroying the whole congregation. Aaron ran into the tent of meeting, grabbed a censor, and filled it with fire from the altar and incense. Then he ran between the mass of the people and the location of the plague. He was willing to risk his own life for a chance to save the lives of otherwise condemned individuals. The plague stopped, rather than destroy Aaron. At the time, these were not repentant people. Remember, they had been grumbling against the Lord's servants only moments before. The most telling thing about their attitude toward the Lord and His servants is that when the plague stopped, there was no sign that the people felt any remorse for their actions.

Seeing the stubbornness of their hearts, the Lord actually provided a miraculous sign as proof of His intentions for Israel's priesthood. He had Aaron and all the leaders of Israel bring their staffs and put them overnight in the tent of meeting. The one whose staff grew almond buds was to be Israel's high priest. As we all know, Aaron's staff budded, but only then did the people begin to acknowledge that they had been wrong (Num. 16:41–17:13). This means that Aaron stepped in the way of a very real threat to save a people who were still embracing the attitudes and actions that got them in trouble. The Lord honored Aaron because He loved Aaron and because He had made Aaron the high priest. Aaron was just doing his job.

Guess what. The Lord will honor us in much the same way He honored Aaron, because He loves us and has chosen to make us His priests. He put us in the position to represent the whole world to Himself. It is, therefore, our place as Christians to take out the demonic *arché* over groups and cities and regions, whether or not any of those people ever ask us to.

I should provide a warning here: attempting to take out an *arché* (or even just take something from it) is considered a direct frontal assault, and the enemy doesn't take kindly to it. If you discern the presence of an *arché*, I do not recommend attacking it without going through a few other steps.

Step 1

Ask the Lord if you should attempt to remove it at this time. If He says yes, then go for it. If He says no, then you should ask why not. This is not to question His authority, but rather it is to find out if you can do something about the *why*. If, for instance, you find out that now is just not the time, then you wait.

I had a time when I wanted to remove some territorial spirits. The Lord informed me that I didn't have enough believers standing with me. He went on to explain that there needed to be at least eight of us for the task at hand. His next instruction was to wait for them. So I waited and watched and gathered intelligence. Two years later, He told me it was time to "prepare for battle." I called a meeting and more than twenty people showed up. The best part was that God showed up too. I can tell you from experience that doing it God's way is so much more effective than doing it my own way.

Once you meet all the preliminary conditions for doing it His way, then proceed to step 2.

Step 2

Ask the Lord for protection during and immediately after the offensive. If the Lord has authorized the removal of a demonic network, then He has already given you considerable authority to dictate how the battle will go. I recommend using that authority to forbid the enemy from even attempting to interfere in any way with you and your team and anyone or thing anywhere in your individual and corporate spheres of influence. The Lord can guide you for any specifics that you might need beyond that.

Step 3

Ask the Lord what His plan is. He may not say a whole lot, or He may lay out a very detailed plan right before you. If He gives you the latter, then your job is simple: follow the plan. If He gives you the former, then you are going to want to know what the *arché*'s points of access are to our world. All of the points of access listed in Chapter 8 for individuals apply just the same on a larger scale. For instance, on a corporate level you are going to need to ask the Lord to forgive the sins of a whole group of people, not just yourself.

Once the points of access are taken care of, you can have the *arché* removed rather effortlessly. Ask the Lord if He wants to remove it personally or if He wants you to command it to leave. Follow His directions accordingly. One little detail: be sure to remove the whole network that is or was attached to the *arché* in question. If you leave the lesser network, the individual demons will try to find a new point of access so that they can stick around. If they fail at that, they will likely go and join themselves to another *arché* in the region that has sway over different access points.

Immediately after the *arché*'s removal, you are going to want to pray for the people who have unknowingly been delivered. Be sure to invite the Lord to take up residence where the demons used to be. You will want to ask the Lord to do something very different than what the demons were promoting.

Step 4

Demons like to counterattack. They will seek revenge for the damage that has been done to their territory. The bad news is that because the Lord is inaccessible to them, they will want to take all of their anger out on you. I have been through way too much of this; believe me, it's no fun. The good news is that you don't have to put up with it.

As soon as a significant deliverance is done, I immediately give all the glory and credit to the Lord. In other words, if someone wants to offer praise for what happened, they can praise Him. Conversely, if someone wants to blame someone, they can lay it at His feet. (Remember, after Jesus died on the cross, He basically became worthy of *all* our praise, and He volunteered for *all* of our sins and mistakes.) Then I turn around and forbid the demonic from even attempting some kind of counterattack or backlash against God's people on account of what happened. The end result? People are freed, God is praised, and God's warriors dwell in peace.

POSSIBLE POINTS OF ACCESS FOR CORPORATE AND TERRITORIAL WARFARE

Demons will recognize any entity that humans authorize. God punished whole cities and nations as units (Gen. 19; Ezek. 14:13; 28:20–22). In Revelation 2:9, He called a particular gathering of false Jews to be of the synagogue of Satan. In developed nations, we recognize corporations as entities in themselves, and because of this, demons will work overtime to infest, manipulate, and gain control of these organizations so that they can be used for their own nefarious purposes. In biblical times, there weren't as many varieties of organizations as we see today, but those that did exist got treated as entities.

Questions to Ask

- What was the organization founded on? If the organization was founded on evil from the beginning, this should be repented for.

- Has the leadership of the organization done anything in the name of the organization that is not right? Have they created policies for the organization that are ungodly?

- Has there been a pattern of sin among the members of the organization? If not among the members as a whole, then has there been a pattern of sin among most or all of the members that have held a certain position within the organization?

- Does the organization have any significant internal, strife-related issues (i.e., political atmosphere, one level oppresses another, etc.)?

When I speak of territorial warfare, I literally mean warfare over the physical land itself. In several passages of Scripture, we see land taking on a spiritual significance all its own. In particular, the most notable from the Lord's perspective is the land of Israel and Jerusalem. He has said over and over again that He will rule from Jerusalem. It is obvious that He is referring to the actual physical location. For some reason, this parcel of land has become very important to the Lord. He could have just announced that He would send the Messiah through David's line. However, He also chose to include the location where His rule would be established. Surely He knew the Jews would be dispersed from Jerusalem in A.D. 70 and that it would have been far easier to have them settle in another land rather than in the Middle East, where they are completely surrounded by nations that hate them. However, the Lord has decided that Jerusalem, in particular, is to be a glory to His name (Isa. 62).

Unfortunately, land can come under special attention from the demonic (Rev. 18:2). The primary things that defile land are idolatry and bloodshed (Ezek. 36:18). Those need to be repented for first. Beyond that, see what the land has been dedicated to. It may have a formal dedication, like a house of worship for a false god, or it may have an informal dedication, like a fraternity house that becomes known as the place to go to get drunk and participate in all sorts of other unseemly events.

A last major concern for land is whether or not it was ever stolen from a former owner. Much of the land that makes up the United States of America used to belong to a number of native groups (the American Indians). Most of that land was taken from the natives by unnecessary warfare, violence, and deceit. To this very day, there is a fury in the spirit over certain portions of the land. We need to continue crying out to the Lord over the land (and its current inhabitants) and ask that the Lord would cleanse this land and not hold the defilement that was on it to anyone's account. I have never known Him not to answer that prayer. He takes no pleasure in the death of the wicked

(Ezek. 18:32). He is "rich in mercy, because of His great love with which He loved us" (Eph. 2:4).

In order to get something accomplished in warfare, I recommend focusing most of your attention on two things: the Lord and the points of access. As long as you follow His lead and take care of all the important points of access, you will generally be safe and effective on any battlefield.

Chapter 12

DIRECT ATTACKS AND COUNTERATTACKS

BECOMING A RECIPIENT OF A DIRECT FRONTAL assault usually requires one to cause or demonstrate the potential to cause substantial damage to our enemy's kingdom. What do I mean when I say "direct frontal assault"? Most of the time our enemy tries to work undetected. Most everybody knows that demons are not trustworthy sources for information and perspective. In order to have their messages more willingly received, they usually try to disguise their identities and hide any evidence of their presence. These kinds of attacks can best be equated to guerrilla warfare. They fire from behind some kind of cover, and they are our enemy's most common tactic. This is the job of the wickednesses (see Chapter 9).

However, in a frontal attack, the proverbial gloves come off, and they exhibit little or no apparent attempt to hide themselves. They show up in all their hideousness with the intent of harassing, intimidating, confusing, and hurting the intended recipient.

I have endured numerous frontal attacks. Usually they

come at nighttime. I remember one night my wife and I were helping the choir director/worship leader of our church pray over the choir room. She had discerned some demonic activity and wanted some backup. So we joined her. I do not remember how long we prayed, but we took out several access points for some really strong spirits of witchcraft. Towards the end of our time, I started coughing a dry, painful cough.

As we left the building late at night to go home, I noticed a small owl perched on my car, looking right at us. As we got closer, it flew from my car to a low-hanging branch of a tree not far from my car. It continued to watch us. I used to volunteer for a bird sanctuary, and I got to know the native bird species in the area pretty well. Wild owls don't usually want to have anything to do with people. This was very unusual behavior. We could discern that this was somehow related to witchcraft. I also knew that some witches in the area would keep owls as pets and use them in their incantations. I broke any connections between that particular owl and witchcraft before we got in the car to go home.

On the way, we started breaking various forms of witchcraft and demonic activity off of us. We also started praying against backlash. We could very distinctly discern the presence of demons trailing us. I remember in particular this feeling of being hunted. Also, my cough still hadn't let up. If anything, it had gotten worse. I don't remember if Wendy had any physical symptoms or not. I seem to remember her telling me that her neck and head were hurting quite a bit.

When we got home and inside the house, we were a little confused. We had done everything that we already knew to do at that point, and the attack was getting worse, not better.

My cough had gone from really annoying to fairly painful by this point. A feeling of fear began to set in (beyond the usual feeling of fear that a demonic presence usually comes with). I could see this cough becoming a prelude to choking and asphyxiation. I walked into our bedroom and looked out the window, and my eyes were opened. There in our backyard stood one of the largest evil spirits I had ever seen. It was at least four stories tall, and it resembled a pale, sickly yellow tree with no leaves. What's more, it had taken one of its branches (more like a vine or tentacle) and pierced my throat. Once it realized that I could see it, it drove its branch deeper through my throat, trying to suffocate me. At this point I was coughing so much that I was having trouble breathing. The part that really concerned me was that I was doing my best to drive it off and it wasn't budging. I knew things could get really ugly if we didn't get rid of this spirit fast.

It was right about this time that I asked the Lord and Wendy what sort of spirit it was. The answer came back that it was a spirit of antichrist. I knew that according to John such a spirit was already in the world (1 John 2:18–19; 4:2–3). I also had heard of them being in the area, but this was the first time I had encountered one. After a fashion, every evil spirit is a spirit of antichrist, because they all oppose His work in the earth, but there is also a much heavier-hitting spirit of antichrist that tends to rule over large numbers of lesser spirits. The Lord also informed me that I was staring at an *arché* and that it was the major demonic ruler of the city that we lived in at the time.

I couldn't believe it. I wondered aloud, "Why would a territorial *arché* of that magnitude even bother with little old me?" I had never spent any real time or effort taking stuff from it, and what's more, I knew plenty of people who had devoted themselves to removing this thing. Surely it had better targets. Furthermore, since this spirit of anti-Christ was an *arché,* it doubtless knew my usual response to *archés,* which was immediate removal from power. This thing was taking a very real risk by showing up here. Again I asked, "Why?" Then I had a revelation from God.

I saw what was really going on. It was scared. Somehow it figured out that if I were left alone I would gladly lend a hand to aid in our town's deliverance from this thing. In its eyes, I had the potential to be a real threat in the near future. The revelation stunned me; it was afraid of me. Then I realized that it had a whole lot more reason to fear me than I had to fear it.

A moment later, I caught my breath between fits of coughing and addressed the monster. I started telling it that I knew that it was scared and that it was in big trouble. At this point we both became aware of something. If it persisted with the attack, in order to defend myself, the Lord would give me the authority to remove it on the spot. Rather than lose its whole kingdom, it decided to break off the attack for the time being. I had found a demon that wasn't inclined to following orders, and it was able to viciously attack me physically. It would be about a month before my throat completely recovered.

The next day I threw myself into the Word. I began researching and praying for revelation concerning every reference to the spirit of antichrist. The Lord showed me that it has a degree of permission to move about in the earth that will not be revoked until God judges it from the throne room and Jesus returns to Earth to execute that judgment. When He does show up, there is no battle. Christ's triumphant return and the Battle of Armageddon are two major events that happen simultaneously; really, it could more accurately be called the Slaughter at Armageddon. It all starts in Revelation 19:11:

> And I saw heaven opened, and behold, a white horse, and He who sat on it is called Faithful and True, and in righteousness He judges and wages war.

John goes on to describe the Lord in very powerful language for the next five verses. Then an angel spends another verse and a half calling all the birds of the air together to eat the dead that will result from the battle. Verse 19 acknowledges that the Beast (a.k.a. the Antichrist) and all his followers had gathered themselves together to fight against the Lord. Usually when two armies in Scripture are set for battle, there is a line that says something to the effect of, "And there was a very great battle that day, and..." There is no such reference here. All it says is that the Beast and false prophet were seized and thrown alive into the lake of fire, and Jesus spoke and the rest of the army died. Oh, and the birds ate well that day (Rev. 19:20–21). That's it. No battle.

As a future strategy, the Lord told me that I should just draw this spirit's attention to its impending doom. More specifically, He wanted me to illuminate the contrasts between the Antichrist and Jesus from that passage, demonstrating that this demonic spirit is really nothing more than a very pathetic impersonation of true greatness.

The same spirit showed up once or twice after that. When it did, it got an earful. Eventually, it quit using direct frontal assaults. In the weeks that followed, I encountered two other people that had similar dealings with it. We never did get to see it taken out, because the Lord had us move away less than a year later.

It may surprise you to discover that there is a story in Scripture that tells of a conversation between a man and a demon. It is found in the Book of Job. For context: Satan has vented his fury, and Job is sitting on the ground wearing torn clothes, covered from head to toe with boils. His friends show up some time later and sit with him for a week. Finally, Job speaks and curses the day of his birth. Then the first of his friends, Eliphaz, speaks to comfort him and basically says that innocent people do not suffer; therefore, Job must have done something wrong. During his discourse, he recounts a visitation he had from a demon. He doesn't call it a demon, but you can tell from his description that this was no angel from the Lord.

Now a word was brought to me stealthily, And my ear received a whisper of it. Amid disquieting thoughts from the visions of the night, When deep sleep falls on men, Dread came upon me, and trembling, And made all my bones shake. Then a spirit passed by my face; The hair of my flesh bristled up. It stood still, but I could not discern its appearance; A form was before my eyes; There was silence, then

I heard a voice: "Can mankind be just before God? Can a man be pure before his Maker? He puts no trust even in His servants; And against His angels He charges error. How much more those who dwell in houses of clay, Whose foundation is in the dust, Who are crushed before the moth! Between morning and evening they are broken in pieces; Unobserved, they perish forever. Is not their tent-cord plucked up within them? They die, yet without wisdom."

—Job 4:12–21

This demon's rantings become the basis of all of Eliphaz's arguments, and the others quickly join him in blaming Job. God later defends Job and declares that they were all out of line (Job 42:7–8).

So let's look again at the actions of this spirit. It came into Eliphaz's bedroom; it brought an uncontrollable, physical feeling of fear; it visibly appeared to him (he could behold its form but could not discern what it was); it spoke in an audible voice; and it lied to him. Though the Bible does not say why this visitation happened, I suspect that this particular encounter was designed by Satan to get Eliphaz thinking in a way that would encourage him to accuse Job when they would next run into each other. Eliphaz made the mistake of not bothering to ask God what He thought of the encounter. If he had sought the Lord's input, he would probably have found out that this was not the kind of spirit that he should have been listening to.

This spirit probably could have brought some sort of physical ailment with it, had it so desired. Satan inflicted Job with painful boils (Job 2:7). I have personally experienced coughing, headaches, and nausea from different attacks. In the New Testament we read a couple of accounts in which Jesus encountered sick people whose ailments were demonically inspired. His response was to cast out the demon first and then heal any conditions that were left over (Mark 9:17–29; Luke 13:11–13).

I know people who have used their physical symptoms as their main way of discerning the presence or absence of demons in a situation. I recommend against this for two reasons. We should never use the events in the natural as a primary method for discernment; we need to know the Shepherd's voice. Natural events can be confusing, or worse, they can be used to deceive. Only the Lord is completely reliable. Also, if you have decided that whenever a demon shows up you get some unpleasant physical experience, they can begin to use that as a means of torment. I wouldn't wish the sort of coughing I experienced on anyone.

If you encounter a direct attack, you have the right and obligation to defend yourself and anything the Lord has made you responsible for. Your first priority should be to break free from the attack enough to be able to clearly hear the Lord. Sometimes that can be difficult with a number of demons trying to get in the way and distract you. If you discern what needs to be done to end the attack altogether, then you probably need to proceed with that. Generally, the attacking spirit is a power that was sent by an *arché*. Usually, the power will bring a number of lesser spirits with it. Repelling the power and its helpers doesn't do any significant damage to the kingdom of darkness because the *arché* can always send another one. For this reason, repelling the power is only a temporary fix. What the believer in the situation needs to understand is that the *arché*, not the power, is the one who is directly responsible for the attack. Thus, the *arché* should be held directly responsible. If the Lord lets you, you should consider going after the *arché* with the intent to completely remove it from power. That way you cut the demonic off at the source.

Usually things are not too complicated if all you are dealing with is demonic activity. If you are dealing with attacks powered by witchcraft, voodoo, shamanism, or some similar spiritual endeavor, then it can get significantly more complicated. Most of the frontal assaults that I have endured have been heavily backed by witchcraft.

I believe that I receive a much higher proportion of witchcraft-related attacks for two reasons. Part of my calling is to oppose the spiritual activity and power of witches and witchcraft, so the Lord naturally brings me in contact with them. I also have a keen eye for it and am in a position to directly address it, even when it functions in very small doses. I believe that every believer should have a basic understanding of how witchcraft works and how to deal with it, because it is very probable that you will eventually encounter some of it.

As we established in Part I, people have a degree of ruling authority in the earth. Witches use that authority either knowingly or unknowingly to invite evil spirits into the world and into people's lives. They deliberately use spiritual means to get things done in the earth. Their efforts can cause so much harm that the Lord commanded Israel, saying, "You shall not allow a sorceress to live" (Exod. 22:18).

Functionally, witches are a sort of anti-Christian. When we pray for, say, a guy on the street, we open doors for the Lord and His angels to come in and minister to him. When a witch wants to get involved, they will cast spells either on or for this person that open doors to allow demons to get involved. The angels and the demons naturally clash to determine who gets control of the spiritual space around this person. Generally, the battle will continue until either the witch or the Christian gives up.

Often, there is a lot of spiritual space between the spirit that is assigned to do something and the thing they are asked to do. Daniel discovered an unexpected consequence of this space. He had a major prayer concern for the Israelites who were then dwelling within the nation of Babylon. He wanted to know something of their seemingly shaky future, so he started praying and fasting and seeking the Lord. One day, two days, three days, went by, and there was still no answer. Finally, after twenty-one days of praying and fasting, an angel suddenly appeared. The angel's name is Gabriel, and one of the first things he said was, "From the first day that you set your heart on understanding this and on humbling yourself before your God, your words were heard, and I have come in response to your words. But the prince of the kingdom of Persia was withstanding me for twenty-one days; then behold, Michael, one of the chief princes, came to help me, for I had been left there with the kings of Persia" (Dan. 10:12–13).

Gabriel had been sent immediately, but the prince of Persia (a world-ruling demon at the time) occupied the space that was in his way. It took a bit of extra firepower from Michael to get Gabriel through. This happens today for both Christians and witches. A group of witches, if left unopposed, can conceivably release enough demons into an area to make it very difficult to get the sort of answered prayer that Daniel was requesting. A group of believers can actually go even further. We have the ability and calling to remove every demonic spirit that even tries to exist in the heavenlies. If left unchecked, of if we just refuse to back down, we can make it entirely impossible for a witch to effectively cast a long-range spell.

When warring in a land inhabited by active witches, direct attacks are going to be a part of life. When you go to take territory from an *arché*, you are removing one of the spiritual allies of the local witch population. Without that ally in place, it gets harder for them to get results from their spells. A demon has to either take a more roundabout path to get where the witch has asked it to go, or it will have to fight its way through the new angels that are now occupying the missing *arché*'s territory. Witches are generally able to tell when their spells quit working. In response, they often start casting spells to adjust the spiritual climate. This usually manifests in the form of more demons being invited into the fray to help put things back to the way they were. The believer usually experiences attacks at these points. On occasions, demons will advise or order (depending on their relationship) the witches to cast certain spells in order to give them an edge in their struggle against us.

Generally, when a large number of witches are in an area, there are a few that recognize that the spirits they serve are in opposition to the God we serve. These witches will actually target Christians with spells and curses. As a standard defense, I very frequently command, "Every curse, word curse, hex, vex, spell, enchantment, or incantation that is having or trying to have anything to do with me, my family, our lives, and our whole spheres of influence I break in the name of Jesus." When praying for protection or commanding the enemy's access to be cut off, I try to work in the broadest way possible. Usually, they will start in the most direct, in-your-face methods possible. When you begin to defend against and cut those off, they will go after the next closest thing to your heart, your family and friends. After that, it may be your physical property and pets. Then they will seek out your associates, acquaintances, bosses at work, or whatever else they can get their hands on. Praying for your entire sphere of influence usually takes care of the majority of whatever is intentionally and accidentally thrown your way. Occasionally, something may get through these defenses. If it does, it is less frequent and is usually greatly reduced in strength.

When they realize that the direct spell-casting just isn't doing it, witches will often resort to more drastic measures. The devil has a counterfeit version of just about every act of God that he has ever seen. Ezekiel had an experience in which God sent an angel to take him, by way of the spirit, to Jerusalem (Ezek. 8:1–3). Once there, he was allowed to walk about as he so desired, and he was able to see everything that was going on in that place. The demonic equivalent of this is called astral projection. Basically, a witch gets his or her own spirit to leave his or her body—which they leave to be protected by one or more demons—and their consciousness goes with their spirit. In this way, they travel pretty much anywhere they want. I have experienced times when witches showed up in projected form to harass me in pretty much the same way a demon does.

The easiest way to deal with a projected person is to command that any angels that are standing by seize the person so he (or she) can't move, and then preach the gospel to him. Tell the person how to accept Christ into his heart, pray for him, caution him never to project himself again (as it's a very dangerous activity), and then have him placed back in his body. If you get the sense that the person accepts Christ, you might consider giving him a little bit of advice and prayer, the kind you would want if you were a witch who had just accepted Christ.

I usually ask the Lord to cut my living space off from the astral and other demonic planes so that witches can't project their way into my home in the first place. For this prayer to be effective, you may have to treat your home like a territory to be delivered and drive out some things that have been there for a while. I also ask the Lord to completely surround my home with angels and to open the windows and gates of heaven over and in my home so that He has the freedom to do whatever He wants. The net effect is a greatly increased population of angels around my house, which makes it very difficult for the demonic to carry out any of their unwanted visitations.

Generally, if the *archés* know that they may get driven out if they continue to bother you, then you can effectively deal with witches when they attack you and live at peace most of the time. The devil won't waste his time and resources attacking something that cannot easily be hurt.

Chapter 13

THE JOYS OF A GOOD COUNTERATTACK

AFTER THE DESCRIPTIONS OF COUNTERATTACKS from demons and witches in the last chapter, you must be wondering what I mean by the "joys" of counterattacking. Well, I'm not talking about evil things attacking us. I'm talking about the church's proper response to being attacked. Last chapter we covered how attacks happen and some effective defensive responses to them. A good defense is only half the battle.

Back in biblical times, when Israel got attacked, they were rarely content to simply repel the attack. Most battles would follow a similar format. The two armies would meet, they would battle, and then one would flee. The victor would follow the loser for miles on foot and kill as many of the losers as possible. In those days, everyone understood that an enemy who survived a battle with you one day could attack you again the next, so whenever they were given the opportunity, they did as much damage as possible to the other side. Usually at the end of a passage about a battle, the authors leave us with a body count (either a specific number or a description of a numberless amount) of the opponent.

Unfortunately, in modern warfare, all we are concerned with is how many of our troops lost their lives. "How much did the battle cost us?" always seems to be the question. In biblical times, the cost of a victory was inconsequential. The important thing was that the enemy was gone for good, so they wouldn't have to pay the cost all over again. The only time Israel counted their own dead was when they lost a battle; they needed to know if the losses were bad enough to hamper their ability to defend themselves. We need to approach every form of warfare in this manner.

When our enemies attack us, we need to repel them and then pursue them until we do some real damage. I am sorry to say that I had a time where I didn't want to fight anymore. During that time, my enemy hammered me repeatedly. We fell into a pattern: A demon would attack. I would repel it. At its earliest convenience it would attack again. Lather, rinse, repeat—ad infinitum, ad nauseam, ad self-*pitium*. Once the Lord broke me through my own self-pity, the battles didn't last long, and they haven't come too frequently either.

So you are probably thinking, "How do I do lots of damage?" I'm so glad you asked. If a demonic power has attacked you, consider going after its *arché*. If the Lord is not in favor of its removal, then start praying into the sorts of things that will either make the *arché*'s life more diffi-cult or make its removal come sooner rather than later. If a witch has anything to do with the attack, ask God to release angels to siege them. The idea is to prevent any of their spells from having any effect on anything. The Lord may give you the ability to take authority over all of that witch's activities and break every last spell they have ever cast. (This can be a devastating tactic.) In any event, you will want to make further spell casting as useless as possible for them. Then ask the Lord to continuously cover them with His manifest presence and to draw them to Himself. Pray for their salvation. If demons have been stirring up the witches to attack you, they will likely withdraw when they realize that there is a high probability of those witches coming to know Christ as Lord and Savior.

You don't have to wait for a direct attack like what I have described before you take action. You can counter at the slightest provocation. If I even sense that a demon is trying to do some damage to my family or to me or to a friend of mine, I will often launch a full counterattack. If even 10 percent of the body would begin to take this stand, the horde would quickly run out of the materials it needs to make attacks, and it would quickly find itself in a place of continuous retreat.

No battle in history has ever been won by an army that played only defense. At some point, to actually win we have to attack. The biblical model is to attack with the intent of not only winning the battle but completely eliminating our adversary. What we need to be aiming for is a more permanent, long-lasting victory. We cannot kill demons, but we are able to take everything from them and render them completely powerless. The full extent of how far we can take this will be explored in the Epilogue.

EPILOGUE

After This...

*And the great dragon was thrown down, the serpent
of old who is called the devil and Satan, who deceives
the whole world; he was thrown down to the earth,
and his angels were thrown down with him.*
—Revelation 12:9

FOR THE DURATION OF THIS BOOK, I HAVE BEEN TRYING
to give you everything I can that will help us as a body
to get to a place where the devil is completely cast down from
heaven. Revelation 12:11 very succinctly tells us how it will
happen, "And they overcame him because of the blood of the
Lamb and because of the word of their testimony, and they
did not love their life even when faced with death."

The blood of the Lamb has given us everything that we
have in Christ. Those who will overcome the devil will lay
hold of the entire substance of what they have been given
in Christ, and they will use it to score victories against our
mutual adversary. Then they will build one victory upon
another until they stand upon a mountain of testimonies
concerning the goodness and redemptive power of God. In

order to build that mountain and to fully push the devil out of his place, it will require a commitment that will cost us our lives. Jesus said, "He who does not take his cross and follow after Me is not worthy of Me. He who has found his life shall lose it, and he who has lost his life for My sake shall find it" (Matt. 10:38–39). The cross is a method of execution. We will have to give up our vision of what we want our lives to look like and lay hold of God's vision for us. The only promise for those who will make and carry out this commitment is that they will gain a whole new life. There is a catch. The Lord may ask for more than just how we live life; He may ask us to face martyrdom. Here again, He gives us a promise that the next life will be something special on account of our willing sacrifice (Rev. 6:11; 20:4).

At this point you may be thinking, "David, that's a pretty heavy commitment just to kick around some demons." And you would be right. If all of this were just about casting out demons, I doubt I'd be so interested in it. Casting down Satan is just a means to an end. Anytime you drive the devil or any part of his army out of something or someone, you automatically make room for the Lord and His angels to operate. The face of someone who has just been delivered from a significant bondage is a sight to behold. They are radiant. They look like they just came to the Lord for the first time all over again, and they often describe feeling that way too. From their point of view, the Lord is touching a whole new area of their life and heart. In essence, the Lord's kingdom takes root in new territory, and with it comes all the manifestations of His kingdom.

Immediately after the devil is cast down, John writes this,

"Then I heard a loud voice in heaven, saying, 'Now the salvation, and the power, and the kingdom of our God and the authority of His Christ have come, for the accuser of our brethren has been thrown down, he who accuses them before our God day and night'" (Rev. 12:10). I just want to point out one piece of this verse, "the kingdom of our God...has come." This is the answer to the Lord's Prayer. His kingdom has come, and His will is being done, because every hindrance has been removed.

There is, however, one little catch. I like to describe it this way. For two thousand years the church has been pregnant with the possibilities that come when Christ has His way in the earth. When Satan is cast down, it is like the baby has been brought to full term and the water breaks. What follows is a very violent and painful birthing process. Christ's kingdom, when it has fully arrived in the spirit, will be brought forth in the physical and political arenas on Earth.

What follows is my abbreviated version of what will happen after "the water breaks." Satan will make one last desperate—and very unsuccessful—attempt to kill off the Jewish people (Rev. 12:13–16). When that fails, he will author a wave of persecution bent on wiping the Christians from off the face of the earth (v. 17). In order to accomplish his goal, Satan will seek human allies. He will find and then support a kingdom that will quickly become a major worldwide empire. Its human leader will be the one we call the Antichrist. He will unleash a reign of terror unlike anything the world has ever known. It will be so bad that Jesus said if those days were not cut short no one would be left alive (Matt. 24:22).

Even this awful season is not without purpose. It will

finish a work that God began in the Jewish people over two thousand years ago. The Lord told Daniel that 70 weeks of years had been decreed for his (the Jewish) people. If you do the math, that's 70 times 7, which is 490 years.[4] The purpose of this time is "to finish the transgression, to make an end of sin, to make atonement for iniquity, to bring in everlasting righteousness, to seal up vision and prophecy and to anoint the most holy place" (Dan. 9:24). During the first 69 "weeks," the Jewish people put away their idols (they have not turned back to idolatry since then), and Christ came and accomplished His earthly mission, which took the power out of sin and made atonement for the whole world. At the end of week 69 (after 483 years), Jesus died on the cross.

I believe that after week 69, the clock stopped counting, and the current church age began. It will not end until our mission is complete. This mission includes the Great Commission and the realization of the full answer to the Lord's Prayer. As we get toward the end of our mission, the church age will come to a close and the clock will resume counting at the beginning of the seventieth week.

The first purpose of the last week is to "bring in everlasting righteousness." This requires the Jewish people to turn to Christ and ask for His return as their Lord and King. Remember, Jesus will not return to set up His eternal kingdom

---

4 The term *weeks* in the passage can also be translated as "sevens." So, plugging in "sevens" for "weeks," we get that 70 sevens had been decreed for Daniel's people. For the mathematically inclined, 70 units of time multiplied by 7 is 490 units of time. Generally, most commentators conclude that those units of time correspond to years. So the angel is talking about a 490-year span of time that can be divided into chunks of 7 years. Some commentators like to call those chunks "weeks of years."

until the Jews gather in Jerusalem and welcome Him back, saying, "Blessed is He who comes in the name of the Lord" (Matt. 23:39). This will bring in the everlasting righteousness as Jesus and all the entire army of heaven effortlessly step out of heaven and into the earth. He will put the devil in chains, judge the Antichrist and his army, and set up His physical kingdom in the earth (Rev. 20:1–6). Speaking of the Jews, Paul said, "For if their rejection [of the gospel] is the reconciliation of the world [i.e. we as gentiles still get a chance to receive Christ], what will their acceptance be but life from the dead?" (Rom. 11:15).

As for the last two goals of the seventy weeks—"to seal up vision and prophecy, and to anoint the most holy place" (Dan. 9:24), and "the testimony of Jesus is the spirit of prophecy" (Rev. 19:10)—with Jesus living on the earth in a physical body, we might not need prophecy again. If we do, it likely won't be in the same sense that we think of it now (Rev. 19:10). I am not aware of a scripture that specifically says where He will live, but I suspect it will be in or around the temple, which will be rebuilt. With Jesus, the Anointed One, in residence, how much more anointed can the most holy place become?

Make no mistake; those last seven years are going to be rough, and I believe that the church is going to endure some, though not necessarily all, of the Tribulation. It will be, as Charles Dickens once wrote in *A Tale of Two Cities*, "The best of times [and]...the worst of times." On the pleasant side, Satan and his hordes will be completely unable to function anywhere within the second heaven. This will make it very easy to pray and get answers to prayer. We won't have to wait twenty-one days for an answer to arrive like Daniel did, because there won't be a prince of Persia to slow our angels down (Dan. 10). Better yet, the church will be a victorious church by nature, having already gone from victory to victory until her enemies can no longer function. That church will be at home walking in the supernatural.

On the unpleasant side, as these days approach, the peoples of the earth will be very deceived, and they will exhibit the greatest hardness of heart the world has ever seen (Dan. 12:10). John 3:19 says that people in Jesus' day preferred the darkness to the light because the light would expose their deeds. We know this to be just as true today. At the time of the end, Satan and all of his demons will either make their homes directly in men or be homeless. That mere preference for darkness over light will become a violent thing. Demons will drive mankind, who will be all too willing to oblige, to murder and destroy any vestige of the light. Their primary targets will be the Lord's children (Rev. 12:13, 17; 17:6; 18:13). Their frustration and stubbornness will be evident when God's judgments are poured out:

> They blasphemed the God of heaven because of their pains and their sores; and they did not repent of their [evil] deeds.
>
> —REVELATION 16:11

Notice the people aren't doubting that there is a God. The power of God will have been poured out very frequently through the acts of the Lord's servants and several times in the form of global plagues. There will come a point where atheism will become extinct like the Dodo bird. Yet the sad thing is that after knowing and seeing the acts of God, they will still reject Him. The majority of people on the earth at that time will actually shake their fists at God in anger.

As for the demons, they will be more than a little angry:

> Rejoice O heavens and you who dwell in them. Woe to the earth and the sea, because the devil has come down to you, having great wrath, knowing that he has only a short time.
>
> —Revelation 12:12

In a deliverance, it is not unusual for the demonic to attempt to show themselves in all their hideousness right before being cast out (Mark 9:25–26). For them it is one last angry, desperate attempt to hold on. If they catch people off guard, it occasionally works. That last "week" is going be the global equivalent of the final throws of a deliverance. The demonic hordes will manifest in all sorts of unusual and rare ways to try to gain any edge over the church. Right now, they fight in fits and starts, and as we covered earlier, they aren't always unified in their efforts. Most of them are very political and territorial in their dealings with each other. At the time of the end, they won't have any territory to fight over. It will be all or nothing; them against us.

The church's job in that short season will be to continue to be a light in the earth for people to see until the Lord sees fit to take us home. Somewhere in the process the Jewish people will begin coming to Jesus in unprecedented numbers. I believe that the Rapture of the church will be the event that opens the eyes of the Jewish people (Zech. 12:10). They will go through a time of mourning and repentance for the last two thousand years of rejecting their Savior (v. 11). The Antichrist will gather all of his army at Megiddo (Armageddon) to march on Jerusalem to make one last attempt to wipe out the Jews (Rev. 16:14). He will be too late; the Jewish people will have already fulfilled Matthew 23:39, and Jesus will respond to their cry. He will step out of the clouds and destroy those who dared to touch the apple of His eye (Rev. 19:11–19).

Those who lost their lives through martyrdom will be resurrected, and they will reign with Christ for one thousand years (Rev. 20:4). Imagine a world run according to the will of God, without resistance. It will be heaven on Earth, a true paradise. Our obedience to the call of God on our lives will help usher in an eternal glory unlike any we have ever dreamed. This is the greater picture of what we are fighting for.

For too long, the attitude of the church has been to endure this life with the consolation that there is a better place for us when life is over. Many of the best among us have said that we can't make it all about us; therefore, we should witness to the lost and see them converted so that they can come with us. Thus, we have this common interpretation of the Great Commission: win the lost so they can go to heaven with us and not go to hell. Let's look at Jesus' general command to the church:

> And Jesus came up and spoke to them, saying, "All authority has been given to Me in heaven and on

earth. Go therefore and make disciples of all the nations, baptizing them in the name of the Father and the Son and the Holy Spirit, teaching them to observe all that I commanded you; and lo, I am with you always, even to the end of the age."
—MATTHEW 28:18–20

The foundation of the commission is that He has all authority. If we really believe that Jesus has all authority, then as His body we will automatically be in a position to confront the authority of the devil.

These signs will accompany those who have believed: in My name they will cast out demons, they will speak with new tongues; they will pick up serpents, and if they drink any deadly poison, it will not hurt them; they will lay hands on the sick, and they will recover.
—MARK 16:17–18

Notice, many of these works are undoing the work of the devil and then casting him out on a one-on-one scale. If we follow the Great Commission and make disciples on a global scale, teaching them to walk with the Lord, too, then we will have billions of people undoing the works of the devil and casting him out. This will eventually have a global impact, and the devil will be completely dethroned. More importantly, God will be enthroned.

God didn't put us here on Earth with the intent that we would simply go to heaven and take a few others with us. He put us here with the intent that we would be His invading army, completely undoing the works of the devil and casting him out by way of the power and authority given us in Jesus. Once the devil is gone, the only thing left standing will be the kingdom of God, with Christ as King of kings and Lord of lords. That is what we are fighting for, to see His kingdom fully come, and when it does, it will literally be heaven on Earth.

May you be blessed in your pursuit of Him.

To God be the glory,
David Falls

To Contact the Author

http://battlefieldmechanics.blogspot.com